FAITH & WORD EDITION
BLEST ARE WE

*Faith comes from what is heard,
and what is heard comes through the word of Christ.*

Romans 10:17

Series Authors

Rev. Richard N. Fragomeni, Ph.D.
Maureen Gallagher, Ph.D.
Jeannine Goggin, M.P.S.
Michael P. Horan, Ph.D.

Scripture Co-editor and Consultant
Maria Pascuzzi, S.S.L., S.T.D.

Multicultural Consultant
Angela Erevia, M.C.D.P., M.R.E.

The Subcommittee on the Catechism, United States Conference of Catholic Bishops, has found this catechetical series, copyright 2010, to be in conformity with the *Catechism of the Catholic Church.*

RCL
Benziger

Allen, Texas

FAITH & WORD EDITION
BLEST ARE WE®

Contributing Writers
Anne E. Neuberger
Rosemary Russell
Scripture Background: Gloria S. Fuzia
Faith in Action: Kathleen N. Burke
Feasts and Seasons: Marianne K. Lenihan
Our Catholic Heritage: Joyce A. Crider

Advisory Board
William C. Allegri, M.A., Patricia M. Feeley, S.S.J.,
M.A., Edmund F. Gordon, Patricia A. Hoffmann,
Cris V. Villapando, D.Min.

Consultants
Margaret J. Borders, M.R.S., Kelly O'Lague Dulka, M.S.W., Diane Hardick, M.A.,
Rev. David C. Hubba, Debra Schurko, Linda S. Tonelli, M.Ed., Joy Villotti-
Biedrzycki

Music Advisor
GIA Publications: Michael A. Cymbala, Alec Harris,
Robert W. Piercy

Nihil Obstat
M. Kathleen Flanagan, S.C., Ph.D.
Censor Librorum

Imprimatur
† Most Reverend Arthur J. Serratelli
Bishop of Paterson

April 28, 2008

The *nihil obstat* and *imprimatur* are official declarations that a book or pamphlet
is free of doctrinal and moral error. No implication is contained therein that
those who have granted the *nihil obstat* and *imprimatur* agree with the
contents, opinions, or statements expressed.

Acknowledgments
Excerpts from *The New American Bible* © 1970 by the Confraternity of Christian Doctrine,
Washington, DC, including *The Revised New Testament* © 1986 by the Confraternity of
Christian Doctrine, Washington, DC, used with permission. All rights reserved.

All adaptations of Scripture are based on *The New American Bible* © 1970 and 1986.

Excerpts from the English translation of *Rite of Marriage* © 1969, International Committee on
English in the Liturgy, Inc. (ICEL); excerpts from the English translation of *Rite of Baptism for
Children* © 1969, ICEL; excerpts from the English translation of *Rite of Penance* © 1974, ICEL;
excerpts from the English translation of *Rite of Confirmation (Second Edition)* © 1975, ICEL;
excerpts from *Pastoral Care of the Sick: Rites of Anointing and Viaticum* © 1982, ICEL; excerpts
from the English translation of *The Roman Missal* © 1973, ICEL; excerpts from the English
translation of *Rite of Christian Initiation of Adults* © 1985, ICEL; excerpts from the English
translation of *The Liturgy of the Hours* © 1994, ICEL. All rights reserved.

Music selections copyrighted and/or administered by GIA Publications are used with
permission of GIA Publications, Inc., 7404 So. Mason Avenue, Chicago, IL 60638-9927.
Please refer to songs for specific copyright dates and information.

In Appreciation: Blessed Kateri Church, Sparta, NJ; Church of the Assumption, Morristown, NJ;
Our Lady of Mercy Church, Whippany, NJ; Our Lady of the Lake Church, Sparta, NJ; St. Ann's
Church, Parsippany, NJ; St. Joseph's Church, Croton Falls, NY; St. Peter the Apostle Church,
Parsippany, NJ; St. Thomas More Church, Convent Station, NJ; GIA Publications, Inc.,
Chicago, IL; WLP Publications, Schiller Park, IL; Rev. Michael W. Cichon (Sign Language
Advisor); Rev. George Hafemann

Credits
COVER: Gene Plaisted, The Crosiers

SCRIPTURE ART: Tim Ladwig

ALL OTHER ART: 9, 10, 11 Jill Dubin; 12 (T) Jill Dubin; 12 (C) Jill Dubin; 13 Jill Dubin; 14, 15
Teresa Flavin; 16 Beth Foster Wiggins; 17 Diane Paterson; 18 Jaime Smith; 19 Diane Paterson;
20 Elizabeth Wolf; 24, 28, 29, 30 Diane Paterson; 31 Bernadette Lau; 33 Lyn Martin; 35
Bernadette Lau; 37 Tom Sperling; 39 (T) Amanda Harvey; 39 Amanda Harvey; 41 Jill Dubin;
42 Diane Paterson; 43 Lyn Martin; 47 (T) Bernadette Lau; 47 Bernadette Lau; 50, 52 Diane
Paterson; 55 Nan Brooks; 56 (TL) Roman Dunets; 56 (BR) Susan Gaber; 59 Teresa Berasi;
62 Diane Paterson; 63 Emily Thompson; 64, 66 Diane Paterson; 69 Tom Sperling; 69 Ron
Magnes; 73 Jill Dubin; 75 Bernadette Lau; 76 Lyn Martin; 77 Freddie Levin; 82, 84 Diane
Paterson; 85 Kristina Stephenson; 86 Pat Hoggan; 87 Jill Dubin; 88 Diane Paterson; 89 Emily
Thompson; 91 Laura Huliska-Beith; 91 Anthony Lewis; 93 Beth Foster Wiggins; 94 Pat
Hoggan; 94 Bernadette Lau; 97 Jill Dubin; 99 Freddie Levin; 101 Barb Massey; 102 (TL)
Roman Dunets; 102 Winifred Barnum-Newmar; 103 Jill Dubin; 105 Dorothy Stott; 108, 110
Jill Dubin; 112 Heather Graham; 113 Jamie Smith; 115 Terra Muzick; 117 Shelley Dieterichs;
118 Terra Muzick; 120, 122 Jill Dubin; 124 Bernadette Lau; 125 Lyn Martin; 126 Jill Dubin;
127 Gershom Griffith; 129 Kelly Kennedy; 130 Gershom Griffith; 131 Jill Dubin; 132 Reggie
Halladay; 133 Beth Foster Wiggins; 134 Bernadette Lau; 135 Freddie Levin; 136 Beth Foster
Wiggins; 138 Winifred Barnum-Newmar; 138 Jill Dubin; 138 Heather Graham; 140, 142, 144
Jill Dubin; 145 Dorothy Stott; 146 Diane Paterson; 147 George Hamblin; 149 George
Hamblin; 151 Dorothy Stott; 152 Barb Massey; 154 (T) Diane Paterson; 155 Louise Baker;
158, 159 Nan Brooks; 161; Daniel L. Grant; 164 Teresa Berasi; 166 Heather Graham; 167 Jill
Dubin; 168 Diane Paterson; 169 Dorothy Stott; 170 Diane Paterson; 171 Jill Dubin; 173 Patti
Green; 175 Dorothy Stott; 178, 180, 181 Diane Paterson; 182 Bernadette Lau; 183 Deborah
Pinkney; 184, 188 Diane Paterson; 189 Bernard Adnet; 190 Anthony Lewis; 191 Nan Brooks;
192 Cindy Rosenheim; 193 Freddie Levin; 200 Diane Paterson; 201 Lyn Martin; 202, 203
Diane Paterson; 203 Charles Shaw; 204 Barb Massey; 205 Bernadette Lau; 207 Patti Green;
210 Teresa Berasi; 212 Diane Paterson; 217 Emily Thompson; 218 Diane Paterson; 219
Amanda Harvey; 221 Charles Shaw; 224, 226 Diane Paterson; 227 Dorothy Stott; 228
Bernadette Lau; 229 Dirk Michiels; 230, 231 Amanda Harvey; 236, 238 Diane Paterson; 239
Cindy Rosenheim; 241 Amy Vansgard; 243 Morella Fuenmayor; 247 Gregg Valley; 248
Dorothy Stott; 250, 251 Freddie Levin; 256 Jill Dubin; 258, 260 Diane Paterson; 262 Barb
Massey; 263 Freddie Levin; 264, 265 Jill Dubin; 268 Dorothy Stott; 270 Diane Paterson; 271
Jane Conteh Morgan; 272 Diane Paterson; 273 Cindy Rosenheim; 274 Jack McMaster; 275
Dorothy Stott; 277 Gregg Valley; 280 Lyn Martin; 282, 284 Diane Paterson; 285 Barb
Massey; 298 Freddie Levin; 289 Randy Chewning; 292 Dorothy Stott; 294, 296 Diane
Paterson; 299 Lyn Martin; 304 (T) Bernadette Lau; 304 (b) Dirk Michiels; 305 Nan Brooks;
306 Diane Paterson; 308 Dorothy Stott; 309 Freddie Levin; 313 Amanda Harvey; 314 Phyllis
Pollema-Cahill; 316 Jill Dubin; 318, 319 Diane Paterson; 320 Anthony Lewis; 321 Amanda
Harvey; 323 Barb Massey; 324 Diane Paterson; 328 Bernard Adnet; 330 Diane Paterson; 331
Anthony Lewis; 334 Diane Paterson; 335 Freddie Levin; 339 John Hovell; 340 Diane Paterson;
341 Bernadette Lau; 344 Terra Muzick; 346 Diane Paterson; 347 Donna Perrone; 350 Phyllis
Pollema-Cahill; 353 Emily Thompson; 355 Bernadette Lau; 356 Linda Weller; 358 Heather
Graham; 359 Donna Perrone; 361 Barb Massey; 363 Dorothy Stott; 364 Heather Graham;
365 Emily Thompson; 367 Bernadette Lau; 368 Diane Paterson; 369 Jean & Mou-Sien Tseng;
370, 371 Dorothy Stott; 372 Phyllis Pollema-Cahill; 373 Bernadette Lau; 374 Roman Dunets;
375 Bernadette Lau; 376 Diane Paterson; 377 Teresa Flavin; 378, 379, 381 Roman Dunets;
382 Randy Chewning; 385 Lyn Martin; 387 Dorothy Stott; 408 Cindy Rosenheim; 411
Winifred Barnum-Newmar; 414 (T), 414 (C), 414 (b) Bernadette Lau; 418 Diane
Paterson/Tom Sperling/Roman Dunets; 419 Diane Paterson/Roman Dunets

PHOTOS: Every effort has been made to secure permission and provide appropriate credit
for photographic material. The publisher deeply regrets any omission and pledges to correct
errors called to its attention in subsequent editions. Unless otherwise acknowledged, all
photographs are the property of RCL Benziger.

23 (Bkgd) Micha Bar'Am/© Magnum Photos; 23 (Inset) Nancy Pierce/Black Star/Picture
Quest; 26 © Michael St. Maur Sheil/Corbis; 27 Paul Barton/The Stock Market; 38 Scibilia/Art
Resource, NY; 44 Myrleen Ferguson Cate/PhotoEdit; 45 (TC) James L. Shaffer; 45 (CL) James
L. Shaffer; 46 (Bkgd) © Tom Till/Stone; 50 Art Resource, NY; 51 © Elyse Lewin Studio,
Inc./Getty Images; 51 J. Carini/Image Works; 51 Jennie Woodstock/Corbis; 54 North Wind
Picture Archives; 58 © Gerrad Del Vecchio/Getty Images; 62 Photri, Inc.; 63 Jim Zuckerman/
Corbis; 68 Myrleen Ferguson Cate/PhotoEdit; 70 (Bkgd) Stephen Simpson/Getty Images;
81 (Bkgd) © Sonia Halliday Photographs/ Bob Daemmrich/Stock Boston; 84 John S. Nichols/
courtesy Dept. of Library Services/American Museum of Natural History; 92 (Bkgd) © Terry
Donnelly; 96 SuperStock; 104 Tom Blagden/© Larry Ulrich Stock; 108 Erich Lessing/Art
Resource, NY; 116 (Bkgd) NRNPNH/Index Stock Agency; 121 © Charles Gupton/Stock
Boston/PictureQuest; 128 (Bkgd) Werner H. Muller/Peter Arnold, Inc.; 139 (Bkgd) Rene
Burri/© Magnum Photos; 139 (Inset) Jim Whitmer; 142 Erich Lessing/Art Resource, NY;
143 (T) David Young-Wolff/PhotoEdit; 143 (L) Mary Kate Denny/Photo Edit/© John Terence
Turner/Getty Images/PhotoEdit; 154 The Pierpont Morgan Library/Art Resource, NY; 156
SuperStock; 157 Myrleen Ferguson Cate; 160 St. Katharine Drexel Guild; 162 (Bkgd) CP
George/Visuals Unlimited; 166 Zev Radovan; 174 (Bkgd) SuperStock; 179(TR) Jim Whitmer
(CR) Robin Rudd (B, CL) Myrleen Ferguson Cate/Unicorn Stock Photos PhotoEdit; 186 (Bkgd)
SuperStock; 197 (Bkgd) Z. Radovan, Jerusalem; 197 (Inset) Myrleen Cate/Photo Network/
Picture Quest; 207 David Young-Wolff/PhotoEdit; 207 David Young-Wolff/PhotoEdit; 208
© Robert Landau/Corbis; 212 Gene Plaisted, OSC/The Crosiers; 213 © George Kamper/Getty
Images; 214 Gene Plaisted, OSC/The Crosiers/Catholic News Service; 216 © Bill Wittman;
220 (Bkgd) Erich Lessing/PhotoEdit; 224 Abegg-Stiftung, CH-3132 Riggisberg, 1995 (photo:
Christoph von Virag); 225 Bob Daemmrich/Image Works; 232 (Bkgd) © Tony Arruza/Corbis;
234 Diane Paterson; 237 © Lynne Siler/Focus Group/Picture Quest; 240 © James L. Shaffer;
242 Courtesy Mr. And Mrs. Edwin Pacheco; 244 (Bkgd) Gene Plaisted, OSC/The Crosiers;
255 (Bkgd) Thomas Nebbia/NGS/Image Collection; 255 (Inset) Myrleen Ferguson Cate/
PhotoEdit/Picture Quest; 257 Lawrence Migdale/Stock Boston; 258 P. Vauthey/Corbis Sygma;
259 Laura Dwight/PhotoEdit; 259 Ellen Senisi/ImageWorks; 266 (Bkgd) Erich Lessing/Art
Resource, NY; 270 Sovfoto/Eastfoto; 274 © Museo Franz Mayer Mexico/Dagli Orti/The Art
Archive; 278 (Bkgd) Alfred B. Thomas/Animals Animals/Earth Scenes; 282 Marquette
University Archives; 283 © Brook Kraft, Christopher Morris/Corbis Sygma, Black Star, AFP
Corbis; 286 Unterlinden Museum Colmar; 288 © Frank Fournier/Contact Press Images/
Picture Quest; 290 (Bkgd) Photo Disc; 294 Brent Jones; 295 Milt & Joan Mann/Cameramann
Internat'l, Ltd./Photo Disc; 298 © Bill Wittman; 329 Myrleen Ferguson Cate/PhotoEdit; 332
(Bkgd) AP/Wide World Photos; 338 © Noah's Ark, 1978, Zeldis, Malcah (b. 1931), The Jewish
Museum, NY/Art Resource, NY; 345 Luis Elvir/AP/Wide World; 348 (Bkgd) © Paul John Doyle/
Lonely Planet Images; 351 SuperStock; 352 Unterlinden Museum Colmer/Album, Joseph
Martin/Art Archive; 354 Lauros/Giraudon/Bridgeman Art Library; 356 Richard T. Nowitz/
NGS/Image Collection; 360 All Saints in Heaven from the Book of Hours, Rome use, Belgium,
Tournai, c 1440. MS.M357, f.14v., © The Pierpont Morgan Library, NY/Art Resource, NY; 366
AKG London Ltd.; 380 © H. Rogers/Art Directors & TRIP Photo Library; 383 (T) Tim Graham/
Alamy Images; 383 © Alan Oddie/PhotoEdit; 384 © G. Tortoli/Ancient Art & Architecture
Collection, Ltd.; 386 © Discalced Carmelite Nuns of Maryland, Inc.; 389 (T) © Mary Kate
Denny/Getty Images/Stone; 389 © Skjold Photographs; 395 (C) Gene Plaisted, OSC/The
Crosiers; 395 (B) © W.P. Wittman; 396 (B) Masterfile Royalty-Free; 396(C) Gene Plaisted,
OSC/The Crosiers; 396 (BC) © W.P. Wittman; 401(B) Bob Daemmrich/Stock Boston; 403 ©
W.P. Wittman; 404 (B) Alan Oddie/PhotoEdit; 406 (T) (B) Myrleen Cate/PhotoEdit; 407 (TR)
Skjold Photographs; 407 (LC) © Mary Kate Denny /Getty Images/Stone; 407 (BR) © Myrleen
Cate; 410 © Robert Frerck/Odyssey/Chicago; 416 (Bkgd) © Robert Fried, © James L. Shaffer;
420 (Bkgd) © Robert Fried; 421 Our Lady of Mercy School, Whippany, NJ

CONTENTS

UNIT 1

WHAT CATHOLICS BELIEVE

HOW CATHOLICS WORSHIP

HOW CATHOLICS LIVE

HOW CATHOLICS PRAY

WHAT CATHOLICS BELIEVE

HOW CATHOLICS WORSHIP

HOW CATHOLICS LIVE

HOW CATHOLICS PRAY

FEASTS AND SEASONS

OUR CATHOLIC HERITAGE

Organized according to the four pillars of the Catechism

LET US PRAY

The Sign of the Cross

In the name of the Father
   and of the Son
   and of the Holy Spirit.
Amen.

Señal de la Cruz

En el nombre del Padre
   y del Hijo
   y del Espíritu Santo.
Amén.

The Lord's Prayer

Our Father who art
   in heaven,
   hallowed be thy name.
Thy kingdom come.
Thy will be done on earth,
   as it is in heaven.
Give us this day
   our daily bread,
and forgive us our trespasses,
   as we forgive those
   who trespass against us,
and lead us not
   into temptation,
   but deliver us from evil.
Amen.

The Hail Mary

Hail, Mary, full of grace,
  the Lord is with thee.
Blessed art thou among
  women
  and blessed is the fruit
  of thy womb, Jesus.
Holy Mary,
  Mother of God,
  pray for us sinners,
  now and at the hour
  of our death.
Amen.

Glory Be to the Father

Glory be to the Father
  and to the Son
  and to the Holy Spirit,
  as it was in the
  beginning is now,
  and ever shall be
  world without end.
Amen.

Angel of God

A Prayer to My Guardian Angel

Angel of God, my guardian dear,
to whom God's love commits me here,
ever this day be at my side,
to light and guard, to rule and guide.
Amen.

Grace Before Meals

Bless us, O Lord,
    and these thy gifts,
    which we are about to
    receive from thy bounty,
    through Christ our Lord.
Amen.

Grace After Meals

We give you thanks for all
    your gifts,
    almighty God,
    living and reigning
    now and forever.
Amen.

Morning Prayer

Loving God, bless the work we do.

Watch over us and guide us in school
and at home.

Help us realize that everything we do
gives praise to you.

We make this prayer in Jesus' name.

Amen.

Evening Prayer

Parent: May God bless you and keep you.

Child: May he guide you in life.

Parent: May he bless you
this evening.

Child: And keep us in
his sight.

Parent: May God be with
you, (name).

Child: And also with you.

Together: In the name of
the Father and
of the Son and
of the Holy Spirit.

Amen.

My Prayer

_____

- - - - - - - - - - - - - - - - - - -

_____

_____

- - - - - - - - - - - - - - - - - - -

_____

_____

- - - - - - - - - - - - - - - - - - -

_____

_____

- - - - - - - - - - - - - - - - - - -

_____

_____

- - - - - - - - - - - - - - - - - - -

_____

AMEN.

The Bible

✝

O God, we will listen to your words.

Based on Psalm 85:9

The Bible

The Bible is a special book about God.
It has two parts called the Old
Testament and the New Testament.
        The stories in the Old Testament
tell about God's love for his people
before Jesus was born.

The Story of Noah

The Map of the Holy Land

The Holy Land map shows places in the time of Jesus. It shows where he lived and worked. It shows where Jesus told people about God's love. You can read about these places in the Bible.

Activity

Remembering Bible Stories

Look at the pictures from the map. Circle each picture that reminds you of a Bible story. Tell about one of the stories you know.

1.

2.

3.

5.

4.

6.

BLEST ARE WE

Words and Music by David Haas
Spanish translation by Ronald F. Krisman

REFRAIN

Blest are we, ho - ly chil - dren of light — are — we!
¡Ben - de - ci - dos, so - mos san - tos hi - jos de la luz!

Blest are we, cho - sen peo - ple of God! —
¡Ben - de - ci - dos y e - le - gi - dos por Dios!

Blest are we, God has plans — for you and me!
¡Ben - de - ci - dos, Dios nos quie - re ser cual Je - sús!

Blest — are we! We are the chil - dren of God! —
¡Ben - de - ci - dos, so - mos los hi - jos de Dios!

Fine

VERSE

1. For our world, — each sis - ter and broth - er:
1. *Por el mun - do, por to - dos sus pue - blos:*

We — are called, — dos called — to serve! —
¡So - mos lla - ma - dos pa - ra ser - vir!

We are here to love — one an - oth - er:
Nos a - me - mos los u - nos a los o - tros; —

D.C.

We — are called, — called — to serve! —
¡So - mos lla - ma - dos pa - ra ser - vir! —

2. For the poor, the meek and the lowly:
   We are called, called to serve!
   For the weak, the sick and the hungry:
   We are called, called to serve!

3. For all those who yearn for freedom:
   We are called, called to serve!
   For the world, to be God's kingdom:
   We are called, called to serve!

2. *Por los pobres, los mansos y humildes:*
   ¡Somos llamados para servir!
   Por los enfermos, hambrientos, y débiles:
   ¡Somos llamados para servir!

3. *Por los que sufren y quieren ser librados:*
   ¡Somos llamados para servir!
   Venga a nosotros el Reino de los Cielos:
   ¡Somos llamados para servir!

With our families, we belong to our church community. We come together to thank and praise God. We care for one another's needs.

I am the Good Shepherd. I know you by name. I care about you. You belong to me.

Based on John 10:14–15

Jesus cares for each of us just as the shepherd in the picture cares for his sheep. We follow Jesus when we care for people in our church community.

We Praise You

Words by Mike Balhoff

Music by Darryl Ducote and Gary Daigle

REFRAIN

We praise you, O Lord, for all your works are won-der-ful.

We praise you, O Lord, for ev - er is your love.

VERSE

1. Your wisdom made the heavens and the earth, O Lord;
   You formed the land then set the lights;
   And like your love the sun will rule the day,
   And stars will grace the night.

Take Home

FAMILY TIME

We Belong to Jesus' Church

In this first chapter, your child will learn that your family belongs to the community of Jesus' followers called the Catholic Church. From the Bible story of the Good Shepherd, your child will discover that Jesus calls us each by name to follow him. Finally, your child will learn to pray the Sign of the Cross as a sign of being Catholic.

ACTIVITY

Draw a Family Tree To help your child think about your extended family, draw a family tree and label the branches with the names of relatives you know, both living and deceased.

Luis Rivera

Julia Brown

Elena Santiago

Mario Santiago

Rita Rivera

Clara

WEEKLY PLANNER

On Sunday

Notice that the Mass begins with the Sign of the Cross. It is a sign that we share as Catholics, no matter what language we speak.

On the Web

blestarewe.com

Visit our Web site for the saint of the day and the reflection question of the week.

Saint of the Week

 Saint Rose of Lima
(1586–1617)

Rose grew up in a poor family in Lima, Peru. She learned about her faith by listening to sermons. Rose spent long hours in prayer. She wanted to join a religious community, but her parents objected. Rose set up a room in their home where poor children and the elderly received free health care. She became the first saint of the Americas.

Feast Day: August 30

A Prayer for the Week

Loving God, bless our family as we begin this day. Help us follow the example of Saint Rose of Lima by loving and caring for others. Amen.

Take Home

FAMILY TIME

✝ Scripture Background

In the Time of Jesus

Shepherds In Palestine, shepherds cared for the most important domestic animal. The shepherd often walked miles guiding the flock to grass and water. He protected the sheep against attack from predators, often risking his own life. Each evening the shepherd led the flock back to the pen, counting to be sure that none were lost. He knew each sheep, and the sheep responded only to his voice. If even one were missing, the shepherd would go out and try to find it.

You can read Jesus' discourse about the good shepherd in John 10:1–21.

OUR CATHOLIC TRADITION in Art

Irish High Crosses During the Viking invasions of Ireland in the eighth and ninth centuries, the Irish erected tall stone crosses throughout the countryside to remind the people of their Christian faith. These High Crosses, decorated with ornamental Celtic art, often contained carvings depicting events from Scripture. The Cross of Muiredach, at the left, honors Christ the King, Lord of the Earth, with scenes from both the Old and New Testaments. It still stands among the ruins of the monastery of Monasterboice in County Louth.

1 We Belong to Jesus' Church

LET US PRAY

I call you by name. You are mine.

Based on Isaiah 43:1

Share

Everyone belongs to a family.

Families like doing things together.

Look at the picture. What are the families doing?

Draw your family at the picnic.

Who else
do you
belong to?

Hear & Believe

✝ Scripture The Good Shepherd

Shepherds take care of sheep. A good shepherd knows each sheep by name. The sheep come when they hear the shepherd's voice.

One day, Jesus said to his friends, "I am the Good Shepherd. I know you by name. I care for you. You belong to me."

Based on John 10:2–14

We Follow Jesus

Jesus is like a good shepherd. We are like the sheep. Jesus calls us by name. He loves us and cares for us. We follow Jesus.

Activity

Write your first name on the sheep.

Jesus calls you by name.

What else did Jesus tell his friends?

Hear & Believe

† Following Jesus

Jesus said to his friends, "Love one another. You must love others just as I have loved you. Let people know that you follow me. Show them how you love one another."

Based on John 13:33–35

? How do you think Jesus' friends showed that they loved each other?

Our Church Teaches

The **Catholic Church** is a community. A **community** is a group of people who belong together. Our church community is made up of people who follow Jesus. We love and care for others. We are called Catholics.

Activity Trace the letters. Read the words that Jesus said to his friends.

"Love one another."

Based on John 13:34

We Believe

The Catholic Church is made up of people who follow Jesus. We are called Catholics.

Faith Words

Catholic Church The Catholic Church is the community of Jesus' followers to which we belong.

What are some things followers of Jesus do?

Respond

One Sunday Morning

One Sunday morning, Sam and his parents went to a new church. Some people smiled at them. Some said, "Hi."

"Why did those people smile at us?" Sam asked. "Why did they say 'Hi'?"

Sam's mother said, "We are all followers of Jesus. Our Church is like a big family. We care about each other."

Soon Sam had a smile on his face.

? Why do you think Sam began to smile?

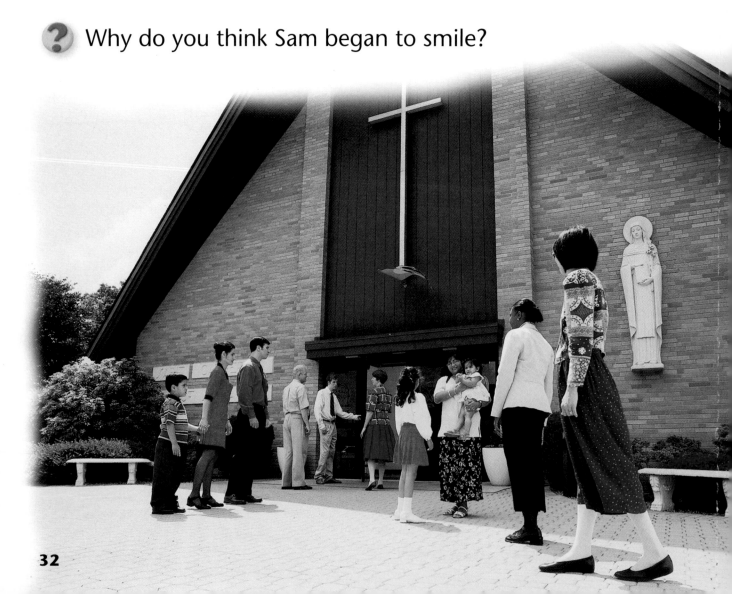

Activity

Tell how these people follow Jesus.
Draw a line from each picture to its word.

help

care

listen

pray

How can we
show that we
are Catholic?

The Sign of the Cross

We use a special sign to show that we belong to the Catholic Church. Say the words and use your right hand to make the Sign of the Cross.

In the name of the Father

and of the Son

and of the Holy

Spirit.

Amen.

A **Circle** the word that best completes each sentence.

1. Jesus said, "I am the ____ Shepherd."

Lost   **Good**

2. Jesus wants us to ____ others.

love   **hurt**

3. People who belong to the Catholic Church follow ____.

sheep   **Jesus**

4. We make the Sign of the Cross to show that we are ____.

Catholic   **good**

B **Draw** one way you can follow Jesus.

C **Number** the pictures in order (1, 2, 3, 4, 5) to show how to make the Sign of the Cross.

Take Home

FAMILY TIME

We Gather to Celebrate Mass

In this chapter, your child will learn that the church building is the place where the parish community gathers to celebrate Mass. Like your home, where family and friends come together on special occasions, your parish church is the place where your faith family gathers. Your child will learn that Jesus is present when members of your parish pray together. Some of the sacred objects found in church will also be presented.

ACTIVITY

"Here's the Church…" Do you know the fingerplay, "Here's the church, here's the steeple, open the doors and see all the people"? If not, the illustrations may help you teach this fingerplay to your child.

WEEKLY PLANNER

On Sunday

Arrive at church early. Notice how the area around the altar is decorated. See what is put on the altar as the priest celebrates Mass.

On the Web

blestarewe.com

Visit our Web site for the saint of the day and the reflection question of the week.

Saint of the Week

 Saint John Neumann (1811–1860)

John Neumann, born in Bohemia, came to America and became a priest. He was first sent to strengthen the faith of German immigrants near Buffalo, NY. He later entered the Redemptorists, and before long, was ordained a bishop to serve in Philadelphia. While there, 98 Catholic schools and 80 new churches were built.

Feast Day: January 5

A Prayer for the Week

Lord God, we thank you for calling Saint John Neumann to build up the Church in America. Help us remember that when we gather to pray in our parish church, Jesus is with us. Amen.

Take Home

FAMILY TIME

✠ Scripture Background

In the Time of Jesus and in the Early Church

The Sign of the Cross   Jesus commissioned his disciples with the words of the Sign of the Cross in Matthew 28:16–20. The gestures of the Sign of the Cross can be traced back to the second century A.D., when Christians traced a small cross on their foreheads with their right thumb or a single finger. Two centuries later, the large gesture (brow to breast and shoulder to shoulder) was introduced, using two fingers representing the two natures of Christ. By the end of the Middle Ages, the present form with open hand was common in the West.

OUR CATHOLIC TRADITION in Art

Stained-glass Windows   In the Middle Ages, illiterate Christians learned Bible stories and stories about saints from stained-glass windows. Scenes depicting events from the lives of Christ and the saints were rendered in beautifully colored glass.

The stained-glass window at the right is in the Cathedral of Notre Dame in Chartres, France. Forty-two panels tell the story of Noah and the Ark. Over one million visitors a year view the windows of the Chartres Cathedral. They are among the world's best-preserved records of medieval life.

2 We Gather to Celebrate Mass

LET US PRAY

When you gather in my name, I am with you.

Based on Matthew 18:20

Share

Catholics gather together in church.
Look at these churches.
How are they alike?
How are they different?

Circle the cross
on each church.
Then follow the
dots to draw
the cross in
the middle
of the page.

Why do we
go to church?

Hear & Believe

Each week, our Catholic community gathers in **church**. We gather to celebrate **Mass**.

Everyone sings a holy song. Then the priest and the people pray these prayers.

Priest: In the name of the Father, and of the Son, and of the Holy Spirit.

People: Amen.

Priest: The grace and peace of God our Father and the Lord Jesus Christ be with you.

People: And also with you.

The Order of Mass

The Greeting

The greeting at Mass begins with the Sign of the Cross. The priest says the words. We make the Sign of the Cross with our right hand. Then we say "Amen." At the end of the greeting, the priest asks God to bless us with peace. We ask God to bless the priest.

Activity Sometimes the people say the words below. Trace the letters. Then say the words.

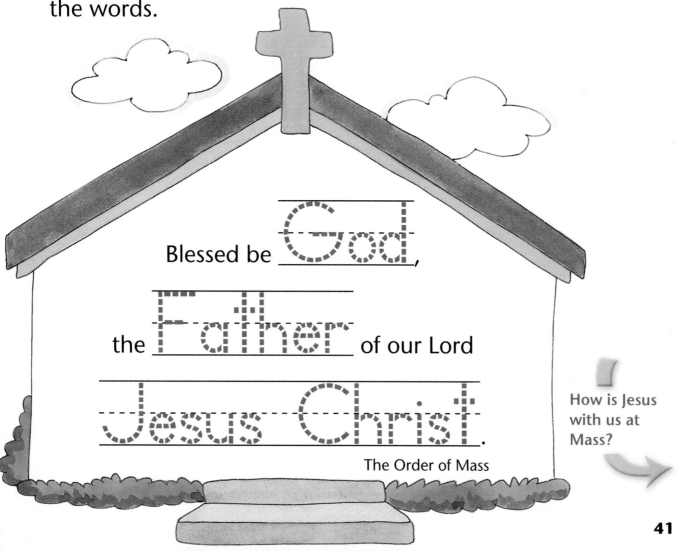

Blessed be God,

the Father of our Lord

Jesus Christ.

The Order of Mass

How is Jesus with us at Mass?

Hear & Believe

✠ Jesus Is with Us

Jesus and his followers talked about many things. People often asked Jesus questions. One day, Jesus was talking about prayer. He told his followers, "When you gather in my name, I am with you."

Based on Matthew 18:20

? Who gathers with you at Mass?

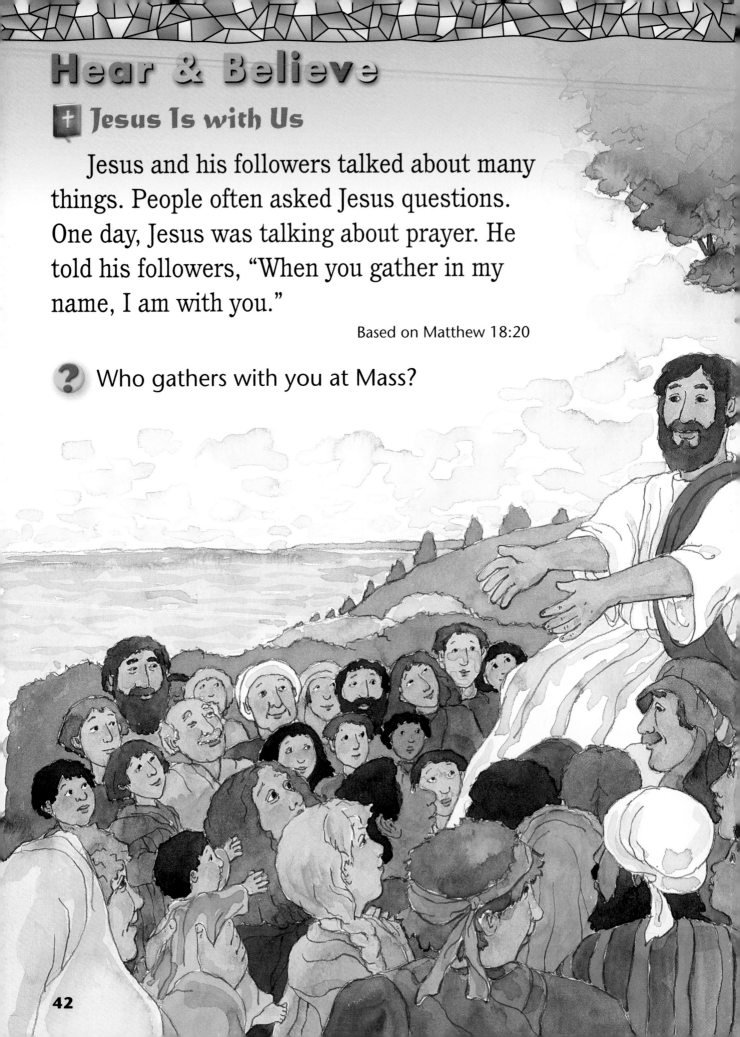

Our Church Teaches

Our Catholic community is called a **parish**. Jesus is with us when we gather in our parish church. He is with us when we pray. He is with us when our parish community gathers at Mass.

Activity Circle the pictures that show times when your family gathers in church.

We Believe

Jesus is with us when we gather in our parish church.

Faith Words

parish

A parish is a group of Catholics who belong to the same church community.

What parish church do you belong to?

Respond

Maria's Parish

Every Sunday, Maria and her family go to church. They belong to Saint Ann's Parish. Maria likes to sing and pray with her parish community. She likes to hear about ways her parish helps people. Maria is happy to belong to Saint Ann's Parish.

? What do you like about your parish?

Activity

Write the name of your parish church.

_____

- -

_____

- -

_____

Inside a Catholic Church

Parish churches look different on the outside. But they have many things the same on the inside. Some things help us pray. Some are used to celebrate Mass. Here are some of the things in Maria's church.

altar table

crucifix

statues

baptismal font

Activity

Draw something else that is in your church.

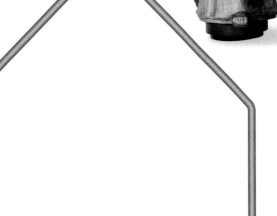

What is one way we can pray?

45

Prayer Celebration

A Blessing Prayer

God gives us many gifts. We call God's gifts blessings. A **blessing** can also be a prayer. Some blessing prayers ask for God's loving care. Others bless God. Let us pray this prayer to bless God.

Leader: For our parish community,

All: Blessed be God.

Leader: For our families and friends,

All: Blessed be God.

Leader: For the gift of Jesus,

All: Blessed be God.

Child: For *(Name a gift from God.)*,

All: Blessed be God.

A **Circle** the words that best complete the sentences.

1. A group of Catholics who belong to the same church community is called a ____.
   parish   **school**

2. Catholics gather to celebrate Mass in a ____.
   store   **church**

3. When we gather to pray, ____ is with us.
   everyone   **Jesus**

4. A ____ prayer asks for God's loving care.
   blessing   **thank you**

B **Draw a line** to match each word with its picture.

1. altar

2. crucifix

3. statue

4. church

C **Draw** a picture of the outside of your parish church.

D **Draw** a picture about a time when your family gathers in church.

God's Word Teaches Us

This chapter teaches the children that the readings at Mass come from the Bible, the book that tells us about God's love and how to follow Jesus. The children will learn that God chose special people to write the Bible and that we call the Bible the "Word of God." They will hear about two men whose lives were changed by reading the Bible.

ACTIVITY

A Bible Story Picture   Help your child draw a picture of a favorite Bible story and write a title for the drawing. Place the picture in a special place where your child will see it throughout the week.

WEEKLY PLANNER

On Sunday

Listen to the Gospel and the homily. At home, invite family members to tell what they would have said in the homily.

On the Web

blestarewe.com

Visit our Web site for the saint of the day and the reflection question of the week.

Saint of the Week

St. Augustine of Hippo (354–430)

Augustine lived with gusto, having a wild life and getting into much trouble. After reading God's Word in the Bible, he repented and became a fervent Christian. Augustine's writings defended the faith of the Church against heresy.

Patron Saint of: theologians
Feast Day: August 28

A Prayer for the Week

We thank you, Lord, for giving us the Bible. Help us learn how you want us to speak and act after hearing your holy Word. Amen.

Take Home

FAMILY TIME

✞ Scripture Background

In the Time of the Early Church

Chariots   Chariots served two purposes in the history of Israel. The first was as attack vehicles, used in battle by King David and King Solomon. The second was as transportation for the rich and powerful. There was usually a hired driver who guided the chariot. The owner, often a member of the royal court, such as the Ethiopian man from Africa in Chapter 3, might read or just enjoy the view. You can read about the conversion of the Ethiopian in Acts 8:26–40.

OUR CATHOLIC TRADITION in Art

Hand-Copied Bibles   During the Middle Ages, monks from northern Africa, the Near East, and Europe made books by hand-copying every word. European monks became well known for copying the Bible many times. Painters, called illuminators, illustrated the Bibles using bright colors and lavish gold to create pictures called illuminations. These Bibles are treasures. They represent the monks' love for the Word of God. They are extraordinary works of art and holy keepsakes of our Catholic tradition.

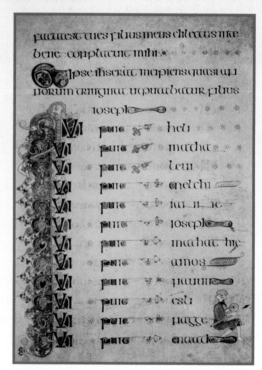

Genealogy of Christ from *The Book of Kells*, Trinity College, Dublin, Ireland

3 God's Word Teaches Us

LET US PRAY

Hear God's Word and keep it.
Then you will be blessed.

Based on Luke 11:28

Share

We learn in many ways.
Look at the pictures.
Tell how each child learns.
Circle your favorite way
to learn.

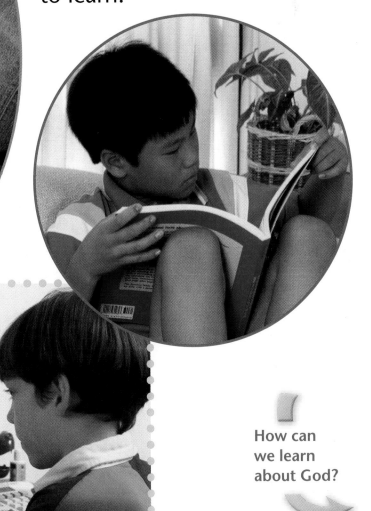

How can
we learn
about God?

Hear & Believe

✝ Scripture A Man Learns About God

One day, a man was on his way home to Africa. He was riding in a chariot. The man was reading his Bible. Philip saw the man and ran up to the chariot.

"Do you understand the Bible story?" Philip asked.

"No," the man said. "I need help."

Philip got into the chariot. He told the man about God's love. Philip told the man about Jesus.

The man from Africa became a follower of Jesus. He became a member of the Church.

Based on Acts 8:26–40

Learning About God

The man from Africa wanted to learn about God. Philip helped the man understand a story in the **Bible**. He helped the man become a follower of Jesus.

We listen to the Bible at Mass. The priest or deacon tells us about the Bible story. He helps us learn how to follow Jesus.

Activity Color the Bible. Write your name on the lines below. Then read the sentence.

The Bible helps

_____

- -

_____ follow Jesus.

How can we hear God's Word?

Hear & Believe

✝ The Storm at Sea

One day, Jesus and his friends got into a boat. They began to sail across a big lake. Jesus was tired and fell asleep.

Suddenly, the wind began to blow very hard. Water began to fill the boat. Jesus' friends were afraid. They woke him up and cried out, "Jesus, help us!" Jesus stood up and said, "Be still!" to the wind and the waves.

Just then, the storm ended. Jesus' friends were amazed. They asked one another, "Who is this man? How can he make the wind and the waves obey him?"

Based on Luke 8:22–25

? How would you answer Jesus' friends?

A woodcut of Jesus calming the storm by an unknown artist, taken from *The Child's Bible,* first published in London during the 1800s.

Activity

How can the Word of God help you follow Jesus?
Draw or write your answer here.

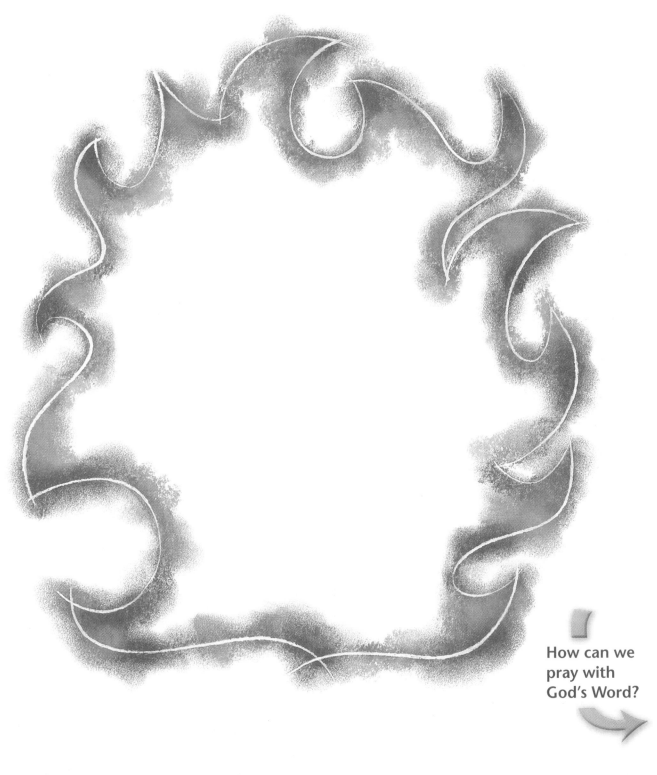

How can we
pray with
God's Word?

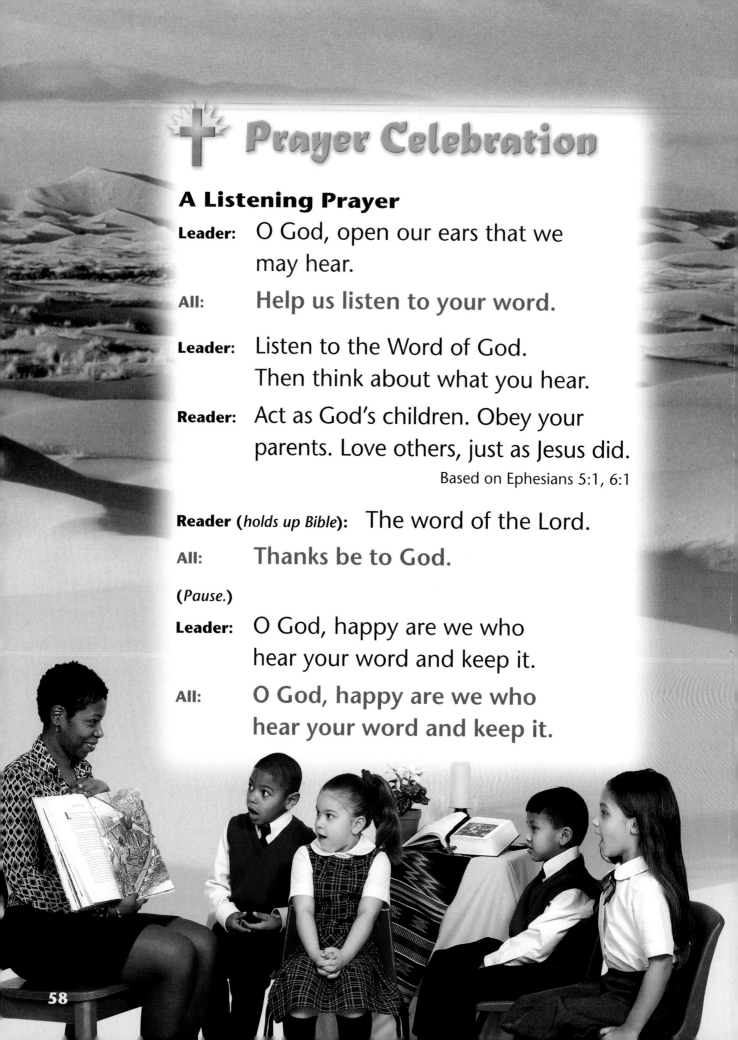

✝ Prayer Celebration

A Listening Prayer

Leader: O God, open our ears that we may hear.

All: Help us listen to your word.

Leader: Listen to the Word of God. Then think about what you hear.

Reader: Act as God's children. Obey your parents. Love others, just as Jesus did.

Based on Ephesians 5:1, 6:1

Reader (*holds up Bible*): The word of the Lord.

All: Thanks be to God.

(*Pause.*)

Leader: O God, happy are we who hear your word and keep it.

All: O God, happy are we who hear your word and keep it.

A **Draw a line** to connect the parts of each sentence.

1. God speaks to us through ● ● Word of God.

2. We hear the Word of God ● ● the Bible.

3. The Bible is the written ● ● at Mass.

B **Draw or write** about something that made Saint Augustine begin to follow Jesus.

© **Complete** the sentences with words from the box.

| listen | Church | Bible | Jesus |

1. The man from Africa read the Word of God

_____

- -

in the _____.

2. Philip helped the man learn about

_____

- -

_____.

3. The man from Africa became a member

_____

- -

of the _____.

4. We learn to follow Jesus when we

_____

- -

_____

to God's Word.

Take Home

FAMILY TIME

We Give Praise to God

Learning how to praise God is the focus of this chapter. The children will learn that prayers of praise celebrate God's goodness. They will say, sing, and sign their praise to God. They will learn that the Gloria at Mass is a prayer of praise. They will also learn to pray with a psalm that praises God for his works of Creation.

Our Family Gives Praise

ACTIVITY

Collect Family Symbols   With your child, set up a display of objects that symbolizes the goodness or talents of your family. Possible examples include a cookbook, an artwork, and a sport's team photo. Make a sign that says "Our Family Gives Praise."

WEEKLY PLANNER

On Sunday

At Mass, listen to the words of the Gloria. After Mass, name the expressions of praise that you heard.

On the Web

blestarewe.com

Visit our Web site for the saint of the day and the reflection question of the week.

Saint of the Week

Saint Benedict
(About 480–547)

Benedict, a student in Rome, left the city to live as a hermit. His holiness inspired other men to follow him. Together they built a monastery at Monte Cassino and lived a communal life of prayer, study, and work. The monks followed a rule, or guide, written by Benedict. By the eighth century, his rule had spread to monasteries across Europe.

Feast Day: July 11

A Prayer for the Week

God our Father, we praise you for all your wonderful works. Help our family follow the example of Saint Benedict by making prayer an important part of our lives each day. Amen.

FAMILY TIME

✝ Scripture Background

Before the Time of Jesus

The Psalms   The Hebrew title for the *Book of Psalms* is a word that means "Songs of Praise." While the 150 psalms, or prayer songs, which make up what is often called the *Psalter* have several themes, they are often personal hymns of praise. Some praise God for the marvels of his Creation (Psalms 8, 148) and for his deeds for the people of Israel

(Psalm 114). Others celebrate God as monarch (Psalms 96–99) or for his special dwelling in Zion (Psalms 46, 48, 76, 84, 87, 122). Try praising God by praying one or more of the Psalms mentioned above.

OUR CATHOLIC TRADITION   in Communications

Catacomb "Graffiti"   Graffiti is something we usually think of as unsightly and messy. However, the early Christians in Rome created paintings and wrote messages of respect and remembrance in the form of blessings on the catacomb walls by the tombs of the martyrs. After a while, the "graffiti" became standardized. Messages from one Christian to another were sent in a code known only to other believers. Certain symbols, such as a basket of loaves and fishes to represent the Eucharist, were used over and over again, and have taken on meanings for all time.

4 We Give Praise to God

I will praise God with all my heart.

Based on Psalm 111:1

Share

We praise people when they do something good. We say, "Great job!"
Sometimes we praise a person just for being special. We say, "You are wonderful!"
Look at the picture. What do you think is happening?

Draw how your face looks when someone praises you.

Why do we praise God?

Hear & Believe

Scripture Praise God!

Everything that God makes
gives him praise.

Give praise to God, sun and moon.

Give praise to God, night and noon.

Give praise to God, mountains tall.

Give praise, people big and small.

Give praise to God, birds that sing.

Give praise to God, everything!

Based on Psalm 148

One Kind of Prayer

God is wonderful! God is good! Everything God made gives him **praise**. Praise is one kind of **prayer**. We praise God to celebrate his goodness.

Some prayers of praise are in the Bible. We can praise God anywhere. We can praise God anytime.

Activity Draw some other things that give praise to God.

What do we do when we pray?

Hear & Believe

✝ God Saves the Hebrews

The Hebrew people were slaves in Egypt. God told Moses to lead the people away to a new land. They went as far as the Red Sea and stopped. God told Moses to stretch out his hand over the water. Then God swept the water away with a strong wind.

The next day, Moses and the people crossed over on dry land. The Egyptians tried to follow them. But God made the water come back to cover the whole Egyptian army.

Moses and the people were safe. They gave praise to God for saving them. Miriam led the women in dancing and singing. They played tambourines and sang, "Sing to the Lord, for he has won a great victory!"

Based on Exodus 14 and 15

? What do you think Moses and the people said to God?

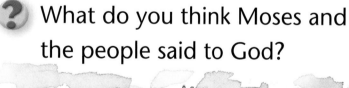

Our Church Teaches

Prayer is listening to and talking to God. We can talk to God with prayers of praise. We can praise God with our parish community. We can tell God that he is good and wonderful.

Activity Read aloud the prayer in the tambourine. Then color the frame. Now, silently pray the prayer.

I will praise God with all *my* heart.

Based on Psalm 111:1

How can we praise God at Mass?

Respond

Glory to God

Joey learned about God even before he started school. He learned that God loves us. He learned that all good things come from God.

Now Joey is in the first grade. Each week, he goes to Mass with his family. They praise God with their parish community. Sometimes they sing a prayer called the **Gloria**. Joey's favorite words are "Glory to God in the highest, and peace to his people on earth" (The Order of Mass).

? Why do you think Joey likes to sing the Gloria?

Activities

1. Learn to sign the words,
   "Sing praise to the Lord."

sing

praise

Lord

2. Read the words
that praise God.
Then use the
numbers on
the crayons
to help you
color the
church
window.

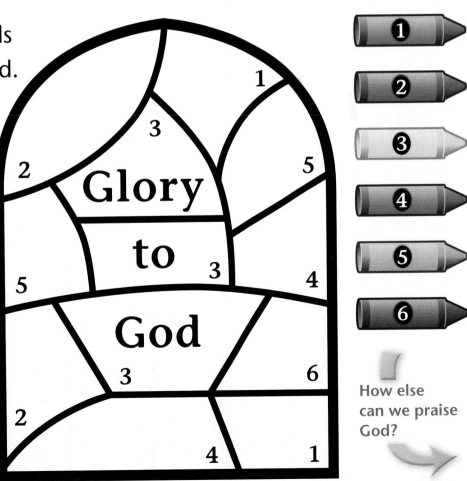

1

2

❸

4

5

6

How else
can we praise
God?

Prayer Celebration

A Prayer of Praise

Leader: Everything God creates praises him. Let us sign our praise to the Lord.

All (*sign*): **Sing praise to the Lord.**

Leader: Now let all Creation praise God.

Side 1:	Side 2:
Give praise to God,	sun and moon.
Give praise to God,	night and noon.
Give praise to God,	mountains tall.
Give praise to God,	people big and small.
Give praise to God,	birds that sing.
Give praise to God,	everything.

Based on Psalm 148

All (*sing*): **Glory to God in the highest, and peace to his people on earth.**

4 Chapter Review

A **Circle** the words that best complete the sentences.

1. Prayer is listening to and talking to ____.
God   **friends**

2. We celebrate God's goodness with prayers of ____.
sadness   **praise**

3. Some prayers of praise are in the ____.
sun   **Bible**

4. Everything God made gives him ____.
power   **praise**

5. We can praise God ____.
anytime   **only at night**

B **Complete** the prayer of praise that we sing at Mass. Write the number of the correct word in each box.

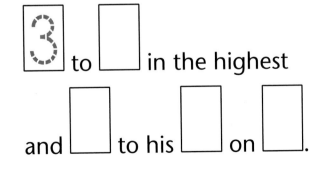

3 to ☐ in the highest and ☐ to his ☐ on ☐.

1 people

3 Glory

2 earth

5 God

4 peace

C **Who Am I?** Write the correct name from the box on each line.

1. God asked me to lead the people to safety.

   _____

   -

   _____.

2. We wanted to praise God for his goodness.

   _____

   -

   _____.

3. I led the women in song and dance.

   _____

   -

   _____.

| Miriam |
| Hebrews |
| Moses |

D **Draw** two things God made that give him praise.

Faith in Action

Caring and Sharing Our Lady of Mercy School has a "Caring and Sharing" group. The children and their families help sick and hungry people in the parish.

Activity Imagine that a member of your parish or school community is very sick. Draw a line from the car to the person's house. Look at the pictures along the way. Tell ways that people can help.

start

In Everyday Life

CAMP

Activity Think of someone you know who needs help. What kind of help does this person need? How can you help?

Faith in Action

Church Decorating Many parishes have a group of people who decorate the church. In Advent they set up an Advent wreath. For Easter they use spring flowers and make joyful banners. The group makes their church look beautiful for each holy season.

In Everyday Life

Activity Close your eyes. Picture a room in your house. Think about one of the holy seasons. How could you decorate the room for this season? Tell about your ideas.

In Your Parish

Activity Decorate a church banner for Advent, Christmas, Lent, or Easter. Write the name of the holy season on your banner.

Faith in Action

Priests and Deacons Men study the Bible for many years to become priests or deacons. They learn how to help us follow Jesus. The deacon in Saint Peter's Parish visits the first grade class each week. He talks to the children about the Bible readings for Sunday Mass.

In Your Parish

Activity Think about a Bible story read at Mass. What did the priest or deacon say about the story? Tell how something he said can help us follow Jesus.

In Everyday Life

Activity Circle the part of the body that completes each sentence.

1. I hold the Bible with my _____.

2. I listen to God's Word with my _____.

3. I read a Bible story with my _____.

4. I tell others about God's Word with my _____.

Faith in Action

Children's Choir Some parishes have a children's choir. Boys and girls, small and tall, learn holy songs. They practice the songs many times. Then they sing the songs at Mass. The children praise God when they sing.

In Your Parish

Activity Does your parish have a children's choir? Tell about the songs they sing. What is your favorite holy song? Tell why you like it.

In Everyday Life

Activity Learn these words to the unit song, "We Praise You." Sing the words as a prayer. Then color the notes in the border.

We praise you, O Lord,
for all your works are wonderful.

We praise you, O Lord,
forever is your love.

Look at the church windows.
Read the directions below.

1 We belong to Jesus' Church.
Find the window that says CHURCH.
Color the top blue.

2 We gather to celebrate Mass.
Find the window that says MASS.
Color the top green.

3 God's Word teaches us.
Find the window that says GOD'S WORD.
Color the top red.

4 We give praise to God.
Find the window that says PRAISE.
Color the top yellow.

A **Draw a line** to the word that completes each sentence.

1. The written Word of God is called the ____.

   • Catholic Church

2. The community of Jesus' followers that we belong to is the ____.

   • prayer

3. Listening to and talking to God is called ____.

   • Bible

4. A group of Catholics who belong to the same church community is a ____.

   • praise

5. Prayer that celebrates God's goodness is ____.

   • parish

B **Who Am I?** Write the number of each sentence in the box before the correct name.

1. I said that I am the Good Shepherd.

2. God spoke to me through the Bible.

3. I told a man from Africa about Jesus.

4. I praised God by singing and dancing.

☐ Saint Augustine

☐ Miriam

☐ Jesus

☐ Philip

C **Draw** about one way a Catholic can follow Jesus.

D **Complete** each sentence with a word from a leaf.

Gloria

blessing

Catholic

Jesus

1. A prayer that asks for God's loving care is a

_____

_____.

2. We make the Sign of the Cross to show we are

_____

_____.

3. When we gather to pray in our parish church,

_____

_____ is with us.

4. Catholics sing a prayer at Mass called the

_____

_____.

Our Loving God

Jesus taught us that we are all God's special children. God has given us the gift of his wonderful Creation. We thank God for all the gifts we have received.

Children, let us love one another.
Based on 1 John 4:7

Jesus went from town to town around the Sea of Galilee. He taught people about our loving God. When we show our love for others, we follow Jesus.

Come All You People

Words and Music by Alexander Gondo
Arranged by John L. Bell

Come all you peo - ple, come and praise your Mak - er,

Come all you peo - ple, come and praise your Mak - er,

Come all you peo - ple, come and praise your Mak - er,

(Last time)

Come now and wor - ship the Lord.

Take Home

FAMILY TIME

God Is Our Loving Father

We look around us at all that God created and see signs of a loving Father. God not only gave us the gift of life, but continues to care for us. In this chapter, the children will learn about God the Father's love for us and for all creation. They will discuss ways of caring for God's Creation and will pray a prayer of thanks.

ACTIVITY

Pick a Card   Remove the fours, threes, twos, and aces from a deck of cards. Shuffle the removed cards and put them face down. Invite each family member to pick a card and to name that number of gifts from God. In other words, if a four is turned over, name four gifts; if an ace is turned over, name one gift.

WEEKLY PLANNER

On Sunday

At Mass, we give thanks for all God's gifts. On the way to church, ask yourselves, "For what gifts are we thankful?"

On the Web

blestarewe.com

Visit our Web site for the saint of the day and the reflection question of the week.

Saint of the Week

Saint Francis of Assisi
(About 1181–1226)

Francis experienced a conversion that led him to choose a simple lifestyle. The Gospel inspired him to follow Jesus with joy, even in suffering. Francis founded three religious orders. All members are asked to help the poor and to see God in all creation.

Patron Saint of : ecology
Feast Day: October 4

A Prayer for the Week

God, our Creator, we thank you for this wonderful world. Help us to be your partners in caring for the earth and all its creatures as Saint Francis did. Amen.

Take Home

FAMILY TIME

✝ Scripture Background

Before the Time of Jesus

Genesis and Creation   Genesis, the first book of the Bible, tells the story of Creation and of God's encounter with his first people. The Genesis account was not intended to be a scientific or historical account of Creation. The authors of Genesis used the literary form of an allegory to reveal important truths about the nature of God. These truths include the preexistence of God, his wisdom and goodness, God's power through which all things are made, and the Creation of man and woman in God's own image and likeness. The truth that God created everything good is repeated over and over again in Genesis.

You can read about Creation in Genesis 1—2.

Our Catholic Tradition in Science

Teilhard de Chardin   Many people think there is a conflict between believing in the Bible and believing in evolution. They believe that if God created the world, then evolution could not have taken place. A French Jesuit priest in the early twentieth century tried to help us see God's hand in the scientific universe. Pierre Teilhard de Chardin taught that evolution was the ongoing work of God. He once wrote that he wanted to teach people how to see God everywhere, even in the most hidden places in the world.

5 God Is Our Loving Father

O God, everything you made is wonderful!
Your love will last forever.

Based on Psalm 136:4

Share

God made all things.
All things show God's love.
Look at the picture.
Tell how each thing
shows God's love.

Draw something you like that
shows God's love.

How did
God create
the world?

Hear & Believe

God made the and at night.

God made the for warmth and light.

And on the land, God planted ,

while in the sky flew and .

The sprang up from the earth.

Sweet and came to birth.

The and swam in the seas.

And on the land were .

Soon and  did appear,

with and , and deer.

Based on Exodus 14 and 15

God's Wonderful World

God created a beautiful world. He created the world and everything in it from nothing. God loves the animals, the plants, and everything that he made. Everything that God made is called **Creation**.

Activity Five things that God created are hidden in the picture. Find and circle **the moon, a fish, a bird, a flower, and a sheep**. Then color the picture. Make the world look beautiful.

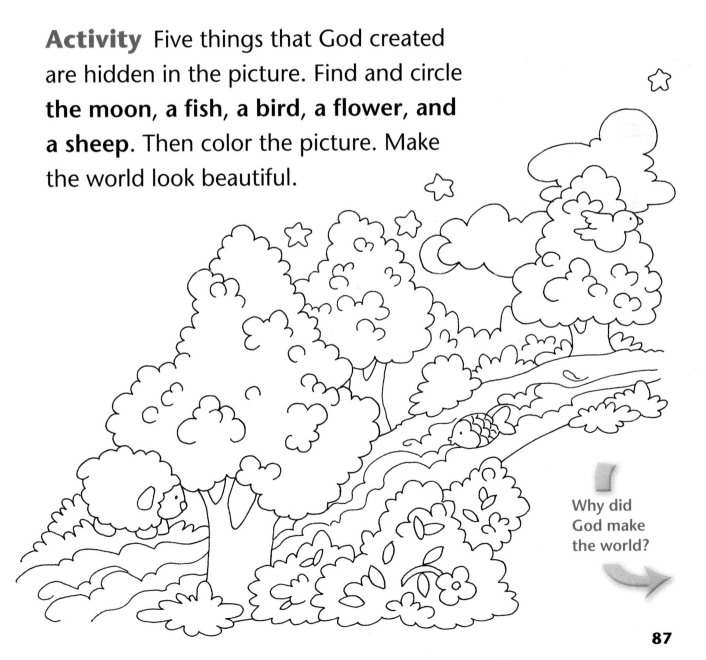

Why did God make the world?

Hear & Believe

✝ God Creates People

God saw that everything he created was good. Then God created people to be like himself. God told the people to take care of the fish, the birds, and all the animals. God said, "The plants and the trees will give you food to eat."

God blessed the people and told them to have children. God rested when the work of Creation was done.

Based on Genesis 1:26–31, 2:3

? How are we like God?

Our Church Teaches

God is our loving Father. He created everything in the world to show his love for us. God cares for us and for all Creation. God is our **Creator**.

Activity God gives us special people to love and care for us. Write the names of people who love and care for you.

My Love and Care List

How can we care for God's Creation?

Respond

Caring for Creation

Anna liked to play in her yard. She liked the little flower garden. Best of all, Anna liked the statue of Saint Francis. Anna learned that Francis loved everything God created. Francis took good care of plants. He was kind to animals. He helped people in need.

Anna picked up her watering can. She said, "Thank you, God, for making our world." Then Anna began to water the flowers.

 How did Anna care for God's Creation?

Activities

1. Draw yourself
in the heart.
Think about
how much
God loves you.

God Loves Me.

God Made Me.

2. Here are some
ways we care for
God's Creation.
Draw a line from each way
to its matching picture.

Help people in need.

Be kind to animals.

Share God's gifts.

How can we
thank God
for loving us?

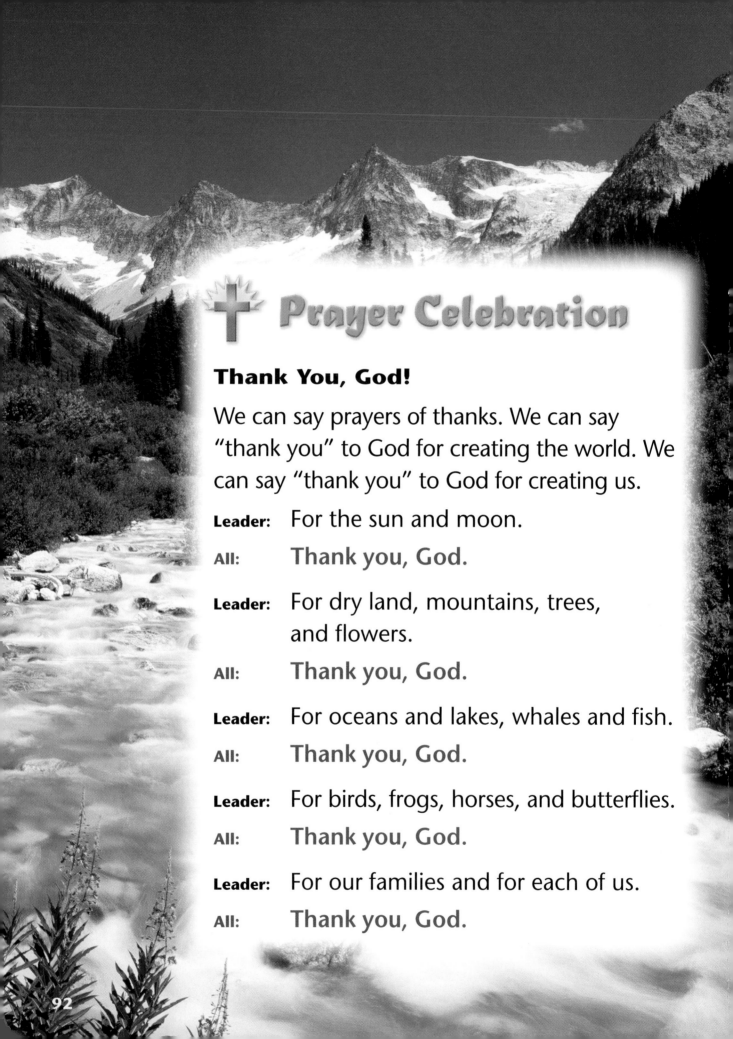

Prayer Celebration

Thank You, God!

We can say prayers of thanks. We can say "thank you" to God for creating the world. We can say "thank you" to God for creating us.

Leader: For the sun and moon.

All: Thank you, God.

Leader: For dry land, mountains, trees, and flowers.

All: Thank you, God.

Leader: For oceans and lakes, whales and fish.

All: Thank you, God.

Leader: For birds, frogs, horses, and butterflies.

All: Thank you, God.

Leader: For our families and for each of us.

All: Thank you, God.

A **Complete** the sentences with the words on the flowers.

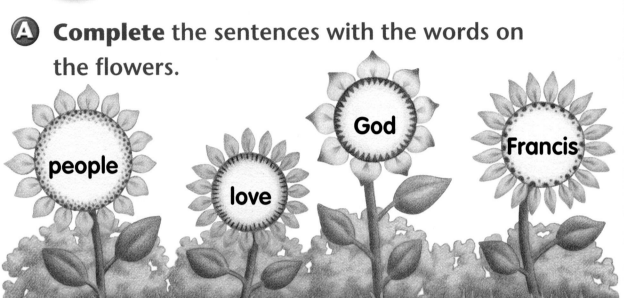

people

love

God

Francis

1. Our loving Father and Creator is

   _____

   -

   _____.

               _____

   -

2. God made _____ to be like himself.

                      _____

   - - - - - - - - - - - - - - - - - - -

3. God's Creation shows his _____ for us.

      _____

   -

4. Saint _____ showed his love for

   everything that God created.

5 Chapter Review

B **Circle** the gift of God's Creation that you like best.

Complete the words of the thank you prayer with letters from the globe.

Th_nk y_u,
Go_ fo_ th_ g_ft
o_ C_e_ti_n.

C **Draw** yourself taking care of something God created.

Take Home

FAMILY TIME

Baptism Is a Wonderful Gift

All Christians have received the wonderful gift of Baptism. This chapter discusses Baptism as a celebration of becoming a member of the Catholic Church and a follower of Jesus Christ. The children will learn that holy water is a sign of God's gift of the new life we receive in Baptism. They will learn that God's loving presence in our lives is called grace.

ACTIVITY

Bless Your Child Bless your child with holy water by making the Sign of the Cross on his or her forehead while saying the words "God be with you." Remind your child that God will always be there to help, and that your family will be there to listen and to give support.

WEEKLY PLANNER

On Sunday

At Mass, listen to the words of the Creed. This prayer states what we believe as Catholics. On the way home from church, discuss a belief from the Creed.

On the Web

blestarewe.com

Visit our Web site for the saint of the day and the reflection question of the week.

Saint of the Week

Blessed Kateri Tekakwitha (1656–1680)

Kateri Tekakwitha, a Native American, was born in New York State. At age 20, she was baptized. This demanded great courage because her own people discriminated against her for becoming a Catholic. Kateri escaped to Canada, where she cared for the sick and taught Bible stories to children.

Feast Day: July 14

A Prayer for the Week

Lord, we thank you for the gift of Baptism. We are happy to be followers of Jesus. Help us share our faith with others by following the example of Blessed Kateri Tekakwitha. Amen.

Take Home

FAMILY TIME

✝ Scripture Background

In the Time of Jesus

Water   In the desert areas of Palestine, water was recognized as a symbol of life for humans, animals, and plants. It also served as an element of ritual purification before meals and in actions to effect cures for skin diseases or other ailments. Today in the *Rite of Baptism*, water is used to "cleanse" the soul of Original Sin, so that we may be "born of water and Spirit" (John 3:5), likening us to Noah and his family whom God saved through the great flood.

You can read about the baptism of Jesus by John in Mark 1:7–11.

OUR CATHOLIC TRADITION in Art

Baptisteries   A baptistery is a special area of a church containing the baptismal font used for Baptism. Some baptisteries are separate from the church building and are richly decorated. One of the world's most famous baptisteries stands opposite the cathedral in the Piazza del Duomo in Florence, Italy. The early-Renaissance sculptor Lorenzo Ghiberti spent 27 years creating the gilded bronze doors for the baptistery's eastern entrance, shown at right. It is said that Michelangelo was so impressed that he called these doors "the Gates of Paradise."

6 Baptism Is a Wonderful Gift

 **LET US PRAY** The Church welcomes us with joy.
We belong to Jesus Christ.

Based on the Rite of Baptism

Share

We say "Welcome!" in many ways.
We put up signs. We bring gifts.
We shake hands. We share food.

Draw your own welcome picture.

How does the Church welcome us?

Hear & Believe

Worship   Baptism Welcomes Us

The Church has a special celebration to welcome new members. We call the celebration **Baptism**.

The priest or deacon says, "The Christian community welcomes you with great joy."

During the celebration, the priest or deacon places the person in water three times. He says, "I baptize you in the name of the Father, and of the Son, and of the Holy Spirit."

Rite of Baptism

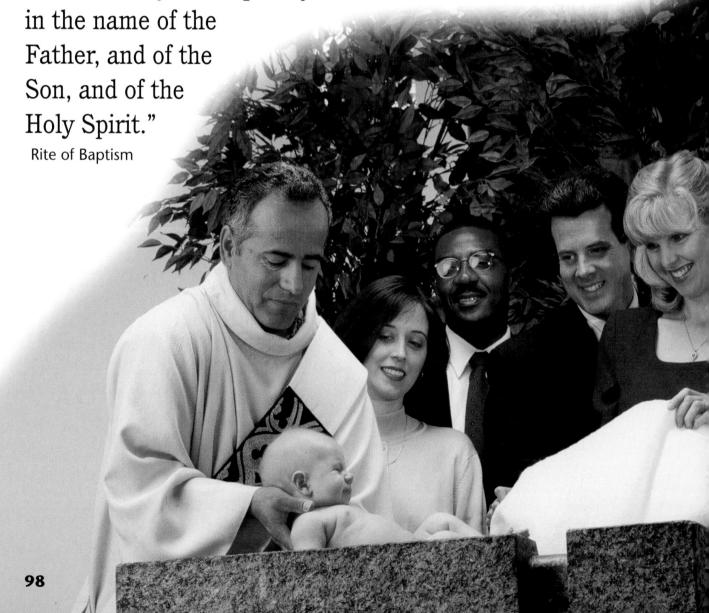

The Celebration of Baptism

In Baptism, the priest or deacon places the person in water. The water is a sign of God's gift of new life. Sometimes water is poured on the person's head three times. Baptism welcomes a person into the Catholic Church.

Activity Write your name on the lines below. Then color the border.

belongs to the Catholic Church!

What else happens in Baptism?

Hear & Believe

🕯 Daniel's Baptism

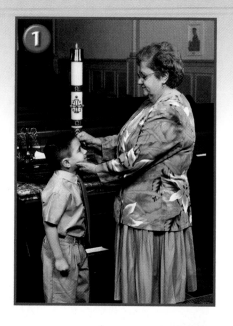

The Riveras adopted Daniel when he was six years old. Last Sunday the whole family took Daniel to church for his Baptism. Father Bob and many people from Saint Dominic's Parish were there. Here are some pictures of Daniel's Baptism. Tell what you see.

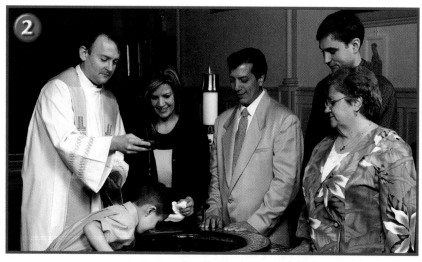

After Daniel was baptized, the parish community prayed that he would always follow Jesus. Then everyone stood up and clapped to welcome Daniel to the Catholic Church.

❓ How can the people in Saint Dominic's Parish help Daniel be a follower of Jesus?

Activity

Circle the people who show us ways
to follow Jesus.

How can we
remember
our baptism?

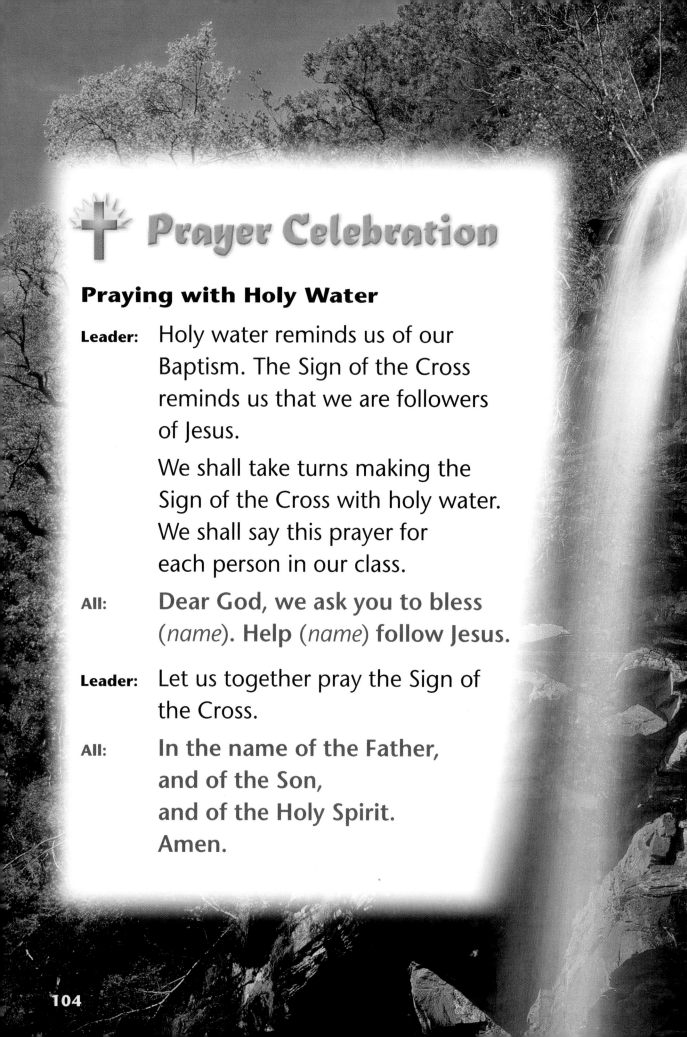

✝ Prayer Celebration

Praying with Holy Water

Leader: Holy water reminds us of our Baptism. The Sign of the Cross reminds us that we are followers of Jesus.

We shall take turns making the Sign of the Cross with holy water. We shall say this prayer for each person in our class.

All: **Dear God, we ask you to bless** (*name*)**. Help** (*name*) **follow Jesus.**

Leader: Let us together pray the Sign of the Cross.

All: **In the name of the Father,
and of the Son,
and of the Holy Spirit.
Amen.**

Ⓐ Draw a line to connect the parts of each sentence.

1. In Baptism, we become members of the • • grace.

2. The water of Baptism is a sign of • • new life.

3. God's loving presence in our lives is called • • Church.

Ⓑ Draw or write about one way a Catholic can follow Jesus.

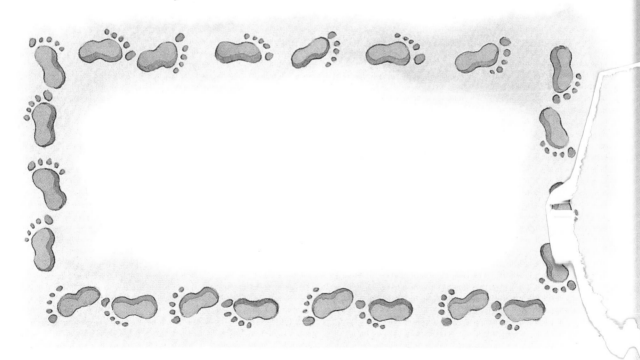

Ⓒ **Draw a line** to match each Baptism picture with the correct sentence.

1.  ● ● Daniel puts on a white robe.

2.  ● ● Daniel's godmother makes the Sign of the Cross on his forehead.

3.  ● ● Father Bob pours water over Daniel's head.

4.  ● ● Daniel's candle reminds everyone of Jesus.

Take Home

FAMILY TIME

God Made Us to Be Good and Holy

In this chapter, the children will learn that God made us to be loving people. By loving as Jesus did, we will recognize God's image in others and become holy. The children will also learn that God wants us to be happy with him forever in Heaven.

ACTIVITY

God's Presence   Explain to your child that God created us and that he is present in each of us. Make a poster with the title "God is present in everyone." Help your child paste photos or drawings of family members and friends onto the poster. Label the pictures.

WEEKLY PLANNER

On Sunday

God is present in everyone in your parish community. At Mass, introduce yourselves to someone you have not met before.

On the Web
blestarewe.com

 Visit our Web site for the saint of the day and the reflection question of the week.

Saint of the Week

St. Elizabeth Ann Seton (1774–1821)

Elizabeth Seton, a wife and mother, felt God's call to become a Catholic after her husband died. She became a teacher and opened a Catholic girls' school in Maryland. Elizabeth Seton became a religious sister and founded the Sisters of Charity in the U.S. In 1975 she became the first American-born saint.

Feast Day: January 4

Dear God, guide us along the path to Heaven. Help us trust in you and show our love for others by following the example of Saint Elizabeth Ann Seton. Amen.

Take Home

FAMILY TIME

✝ Scripture Background

In the Time of Jesus

Scribes   Scribes were Jewish men capable of reading and writing, who were experts in Mosaic Law. They studied the Hebrew Scriptures, since they contained so much of the law of Israel. In the New Testament, scribes are often seen confronting Jesus on questions of the Law. A scribe, who questions Jesus in Luke's Gospel, demonstrates his knowledge of the Books of Leviticus and Deuteronomy, where the Great Commandment is first found.

You can read about the scribe's question in Luke 10:25–28 and about the Law in Leviticus 19:18 and Deuteronomy 6:5.

OUR CATHOLIC TRADITION   in Holy People

Saints   The Church has canonized, or declared certain good and holy people saints. Many saints had ordinary lives. It was not unusual for these good and holy people to be dismissed by family, friends, and even church officials during much of their lifetime. For some, their good works were only acknowledged after their deaths.

All the saints had one thing in common. They lived out the Great Commandment by showing their steadfast love for God and by loving their neighbor as they loved themselves.

A tenth-century Byzantine ivory triptych of saints

7 God Made Us to Be Good and Holy

Children, let us love one another.

Based on 1 John 4:7

Share

Everything has a purpose.
Circle the things that you would
use in a playhouse.
Why did
you choose
each thing?

Draw one
more thing
to put in a
playhouse.

Why did God
create us?

✝ Scripture A Man Questions Jesus

Jesus went from town to town teaching the people. One day, a man who knew God's Law asked Jesus a question.

Man: What must I do to go to Heaven?

Jesus (*smiling*): What is written in the Bible?

Man: Love God with your whole heart and with your whole mind. Love others as you love yourself.

Jesus: You are right. That is why God made you. That is what you must do to go to Heaven.

Based on Luke 10:25–28

Our Church Teaches

God created us to love him, ourselves, and other people. God made us to be happy with him forever in Heaven.

Someday every living thing will die. But death is not the end. If we love God and others, we will live forever. We will be with Jesus. We will be with all the good and holy people who ever lived. This will be the happiness of Heaven.

Activity Circle three letters hidden in the picture. Use the letters to complete the words in the sentences below. Read how you can show love for God and others.

I can _hare.
I can _are.
I can _ray.

How else can we be good and holy?

Respond

A Holy Man Named Peter

Peter could not think as fast as other people. He spoke very slowly. He walked with a limp. Some people made fun of Peter. But Peter always smiled back.

Peter liked people. He wanted to help them. That is why he liked his job at the grocery store. Peter packed the bags. Then he helped carry them out to the cars.

Peter listened to people's problems. He told the people that God loves them. Peter helped many people feel better.

When Peter died, people were very sad. They said, "Peter was a good and holy man. We were happy to know him."

 How was Peter good and holy?

Activity

Play the game about loving God and other people. Find your way to Jesus.

1. Each player needs a game marker.

2. Toss a penny.

3. Move 1 space for heads or 2 for tails.

Start

You prayed. 1 Go 1 more space.

2

You shared. 3 Go 1 more space.

4

You cared. 5 Go 1 more space.

6

You thanked God. 9 Go 1 more space.

8

You helped. 7 Go 1 more space.

Toss heads. 10 Go to Jesus.

Jesus

How can we celebrate being good and holy?

✝ Prayer Celebration

Praying with Movement

Prayer helps us to be good and holy. Moving our bodies can help us pray. The words and music of holy songs can help us move.

Let us move our bodies to the words and music of a holy song.

Chapter Review

A **Write** the number of the correct word in each box. The first one is done for you.

1. God made us to be ⟨3⟩ and ⟨ ⟩.

2. To be holy is to be like ⟨ ⟩.

3. Jesus tells us to ⟨ ⟩ God, ourselves, and other people.

4. If we do this, we will be ⟨ ⟩ with God forever in ⟨ ⟩.

B **Write** the number of each picture before the correct word.

☐ share   ☐ care   ☐ pray   ☐ help

C **Write or draw** about one way Elizabeth Ann Seton showed love for others.

Take Home

FAMILY TIME

We Give Thanks to God

God, our loving Father, gives us so much to be thankful for. In this chapter, the children will identify some of God's special gifts. They will learn why we refer to God as "our Father," and that his name is holy. They will experience thanking God with their hearts and with their voices.

OUR FAMILY

ACTIVITY

Thanksgiving   A cornucopia, the horn-shaped basket filled with fruits and vegetables, represents the bounty we receive from the earth—from the goodness of the land God created. Tape a piece of construction paper in the shape of a cornucopia. Then fill it with fruit and vegetable shapes cut out of paper. Write something you and your child are thankful for on each shape.

WEEKLY PLANNER

On Sunday

The word *Eucharist* means "thanks," and the Mass is a prayer of thanksgiving. Have a thankful heart when you come to the Liturgy this Sunday.

On the Web

blestarewe.com

Visit our Web site for the saint of the day and the reflection question of the week.

Saint of the Week

 Saint Isidore the Farmer (1080–1130)

Isidore spent much of his life working on a farm in Spain. He and his wife Maria, also a saint, showed their love for God by being kind to their neighbors. Although poor, Isidore and Maria shared their food with those poorer than themselves.

Patron Saint of: farmers and migrant workers
Feast Day: May 15

A Prayer for the Week

God our Father, we thank you for all your gifts. Help us follow the example of Saint Isidore by praying each day, by working hard, and by sharing our food with the poor. Amen.

Take Home

FAMILY TIME

✝ Scripture Background

In the Time of Jesus

Our Father Jesus revealed that God is our heavenly Father. When praying to his Father, Jesus used the Aramaic term "abba," a more intimate form of the word "father," much like "dad" in our language. Jesus wants us to have a similar relationship with God, who as a loving Father looks after his children and knows what they need. We pray as Jesus taught us when we say "Our Father" with all those baptized in the name of the Trinity.

You can read about praying to God the Father in Matthew 6:6–15 and 7:7–11. Then slowly pray the Lord's Prayer.

OUR CATHOLIC TRADITION in Music

A Hymn of Thanks A well-known hymn of thanksgiving is "Now Thank We All Our God." The lyrics, based on Sirach 50:20–24, were originally written in German by Martin Rinkart under the title of "Nun danket alle Gott." The hymn probably first appeared in 1636. The hymn's composer, Johann Crüger, led the choir at St. Nicholas (Lutheran) Church in Berlin during the seventeenth century. He composed some of the finest hymn tunes of all times. Catherine Winkworth published her English translation of the hymn in 1858. Today "Now Thank We All Our God" is sung in many Catholic parishes on Thanksgiving Day.

Nun danket alle Gott

Nun dan–ket al–le Gott mit Her–zen, Mund und
Hän–den, der gro–sse Din–ge tut an uns und al–len
En–den, der uns von Mut–ter–leib und Kin–des–bei–nen
an un–zäh–lig viel zu–gut und noch jetz–und ge–tan.

Words: Nun danket alle Gott, Martin Rinkart, 1586-1649
Music: NUN DANKET, Johann Crüger, 1598-1662; harm. by Margaret W. Mealy, b. 1922 © 1981, GIA Publications

8 We Give Thanks to God

Thank you, God, for your goodness.
We bless your name.

Based on Psalm 100:4

Share

Aunt Pat helped Nick
and Jenny bake cupcakes.
She said they could put
on the frosting. Nick and
Jenny surprised Aunt Pat.

Color the letters on
the cupcakes. How did
Nick and Jenny surprise
Aunt Pat?

Why does
God give
us gifts?

Hear & Believe

✝ Scripture God Is a Good Father

One day, Jesus told some people about God.

Jesus: God is like a good father. Imagine that you are a child. You are hungry. You ask your father for a loaf of bread. Will a good father give you a stone?

People: No!

Jesus: What will a good father give you?

People: A loaf of bread.

Jesus: That's right. Now pretend that you ask your father for a fish. Will a good father give you a snake?

People: No!

Jesus: What will a good father give you?

People: A fish.

Jesus: That's right. A good father knows how to give his children what they need. So too, God knows everything you need. God gives good gifts to everyone.

Based on Matthew 7:9–11

God Cares for Us

Jesus told the people that God is like a good father. God knows what everyone needs. He takes care of everyone. God wants us to pray for the things we need. Then God will give us what is good.

Activity Complete the sentence.

Jesus taught us that God is like a

_____

- -

_____ .

When do Catholics give thanks to God?

123

Hear & Believe

We Give Thanks at Mass

Erin and her family are on their way to Saint Francis Church.

Along the way, Erin's father says, "God loves everyone. God takes care of us and gives us what we need."

"That's right," says Erin's mother. "And we should give thanks to God at Mass."

"I know," says her brother Andrew. "So let's think of three things that we can thank God for today."

? What do you think Erin and her family thanked God for?

Our Church Teaches

Jesus taught us how to pray. He told us to call God our Father. In the **Lord's Prayer**, we say "Our Father who art in heaven, **hallowed** be thy name." We tell God that his name is holy.

Activity Think about three things you want to thank God for at Mass. Draw or write about one of them.

We Believe

God loves everyone in the world. When we pray, we call God our Father.

Faith Words

Lord's Prayer
The Lord's Prayer is the prayer that Jesus taught us.

hallowed
The word *hallowed* means "holy."

How do we show thanks for God's gifts?

Respond

✝ The Man Who Said "Thank You"

One day, Jesus met ten people who had a sickness called leprosy. Jesus wanted to show the lepers that God loved them.

So Jesus said, "Go to the priests. Your sickness will go away."

All ten lepers did as Jesus said. Along the way, all ten got better. Their leprosy was gone! Nine of them ran off happy. But one man went back to Jesus.

"Thank you," the man said. "I will never forget this wonderful gift."

Then Jesus said, "Go, your faith has saved you."

Based on Luke 17:11–19

❓ Why was Jesus happy to see the man?

126

Activities

1. Trace the letters to complete the prayer.

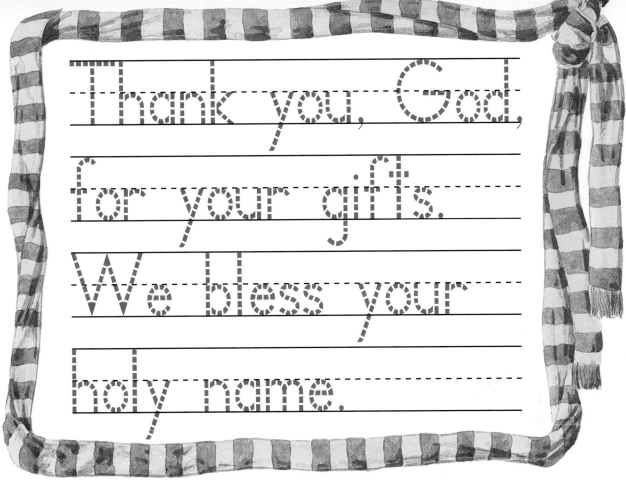

Thank you, God,

for your gifts.

We bless your

holy name.

2. Draw one gift God has given you.

How can we say "thank you" to God?

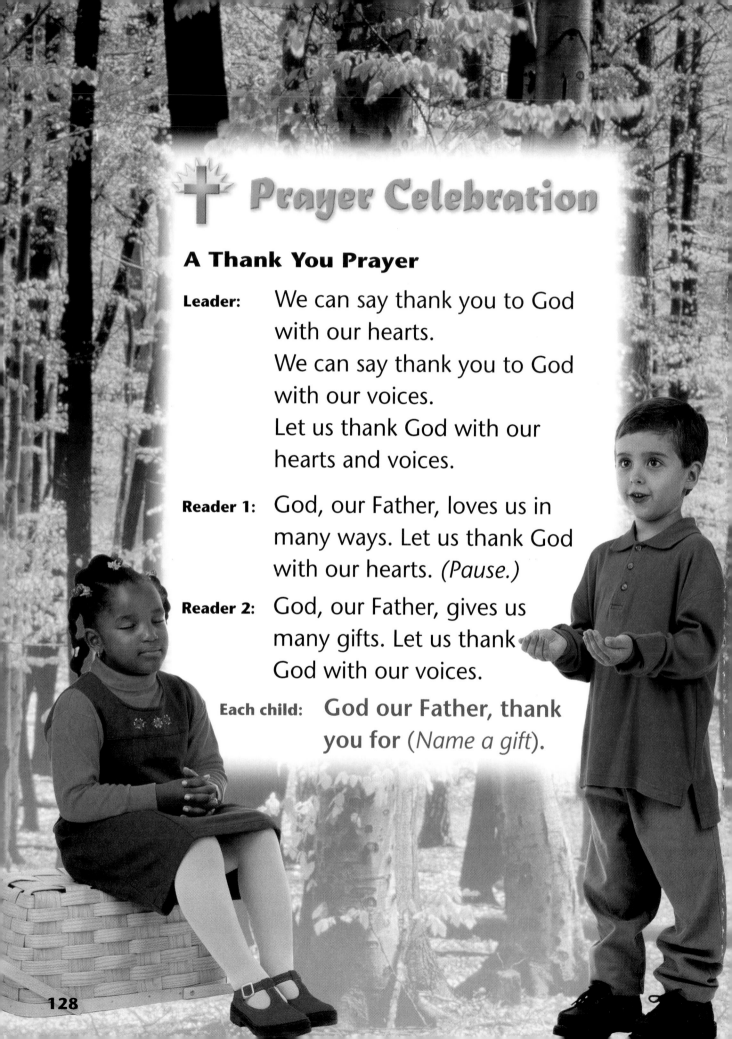

✝ Prayer Celebration

A Thank You Prayer

Leader: We can say thank you to God with our hearts.
We can say thank you to God with our voices.
Let us thank God with our hearts and voices.

Reader 1: God, our Father, loves us in many ways. Let us thank God with our hearts. *(Pause.)*

Reader 2: God, our Father, gives us many gifts. Let us thank God with our voices.

Each child: God our Father, thank you for *(Name a gift).*

A **Circle** the words that best complete the sentences.

1. God takes care of ____.
   some people   **everyone**

2. We give ____ to God for his gifts.
   thanks   **money**

3. We should ____ for the things we need.
   cry   **pray**

B **Draw or write** about a special gift God has given you.

C **Draw a line** to connect the parts of each sentence.

1. Jesus taught us to pray ● ● holy.

2. Hallowed means ● ● father.

3. We thank God with ● ● the Lord's
our hearts and Prayer.

4. God is like a good ● ● voices.

D **Draw or write** about the leper who came back to see Jesus.

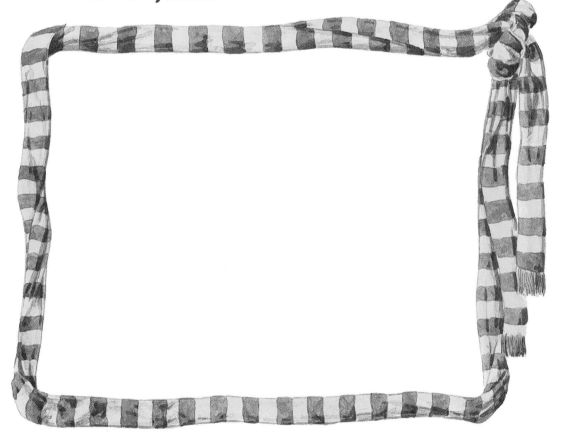

Faith in Action

Church Groundskeepers All Saints Parish invites the children in the parish school to take care of one of the church gardens. Some children plant flowers. Some water the plants. Others get rid of the weeds. All those who help show their love for God and his Creation.

In Your Parish

Activity Picture the grounds around your parish church and school. What things do you see that were created by God? Tell how the children in your school could care for God's Creation.

In Everyday Life

Activity Each day, we make choices. Some choices help God's Creation. Some choices hurt it. Circle the choices that help God's Creation.

Faith in Action

Welcoming New Members Each month, Saint Paul's Parish welcomes its new members. After Mass, the welcome group serves coffee and snacks. Everyone gets to meet the new members. They talk about the parish. They talk about their families. They talk about helping others.

In Your Parish

Activity Make a welcome sign for your church. Draw pictures of people in your parish. Show how your parish is special.

Welcome

In Everyday Life

Activity Think about a time when you felt left out. How could you help a new child feel welcome in your school or neighborhood?

Faith in Action

Parish Greeters One Sunday a month, families from Saint Ann's School greet the people going into church. The greeters are friendly. They make the children feel special. Visitors always feel welcome.

In Your Parish

Activity How do the greeters in your parish make you feel special? How can you help make your parish a friendly place?

In Everyday Life

Activity God loves you very much. He wants you to love yourself. Then you will be able to love others. Draw a picture of yourself. Then pray the prayer around your picture.

God, I know that you love me. Help me to love myself and other people.

Faith in Action

Midnight Run Some parishes collect food and clothes for homeless people in New York City. Homeless people do not have a home to sleep in. Many live on the street or in a park. During the year, members of the Midnight Run group drive into the city to give the food and clothes to the homeless.

In Your Parish

Activity Circle the things that you think homeless people need. Draw a line under two things that you would like to give a homeless person.

In Everyday Life

Activity Close your eyes and picture the things that you have. As you see some of your favorite things, silently pray, "Thank-you, God."

Write the word from the bow that completes each sentence.

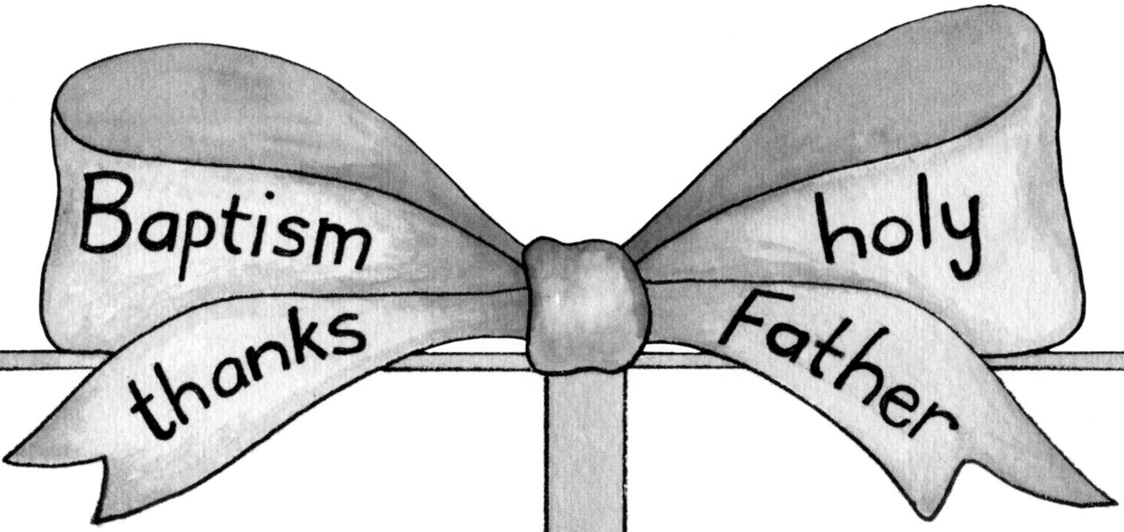

Baptism

thanks

holy

Father

God is our loving

_____

- - - - - - - - - - - - - - -

_____ .

_____

- - - - - - - - - - - - - - -

_____

is a wonderful gift.

God made us
to be good and

_____

- - - - - - - - - - - - - - -

_____ .

We give

_____

- - - - - - - - - - - - - - -

_____

to God.

Unit Review

2

A **Write** the correct word on each line.

1. Who told us to love God, ourselves, and others?

_____

- -

_____

2. What makes us children of God?

_____

- -

_____

3. Who does God make like himself?

_____

- -

_____

4. What does the word *hallowed* mean?

_____

- -

_____

B **Circle** the correct words to complete the sentences.

1. Everything that God made is called ____.
   Creation   **the Earth**

2. The celebration of ____ welcomes us into the Catholic Church.
   Mass   **Baptism**

3. God's loving presence in our lives is called ____.
   grace   **peace**

4. Happiness with God forever will be ____.
   Heaven   **community**

5. Jesus taught us to pray the ____.
   Sign of the Cross   **Lord's Prayer**

C **Draw** one way you can care for God's Creation.

D **Who Am I?** Write the number of each sentence in the correct box.

1. I took good care of plants and animals.

   ☐ Blessed Kateri Tekakwitha

2. I started the Sisters of Charity in America.

   ☐ the leper

3. I taught other Native Americans about Jesus.

   ☐ Saint Francis

4. I came back to thank Jesus for making me well.

   ☐ Saint Elizabeth Ann Seton

God's Son, Jesus

God's greatest gift to us is his Son, Jesus. Jesus showed us how to be a child of God. Jesus taught us how to care about one another.

Mary and her husband, Joseph, had to travel to the town of Bethlehem.
Based on Luke 2:1–7

Mary and Joseph traveled to Bethlehem on a road like this one. Jesus was born in Bethlehem. We can celebrate the birth of Jesus with prayer.

He Came Down

Traditional from Cameroon
Transcribed and Arranged by John L. Bell

He came down that we may have *love;

He came down that we may have love;

He came down that we may have love,

Cantor Why did he come?

Hal - le - lu - jah for ev - er - more.

Substitute peace, joy, hope, life, etc.

Jesus Is God's Son

In this chapter, the children will hear the Gospel story of the Annunciation. They will learn that the Angel Gabriel announced to Mary the good news that she would be the mother of God's Son, Jesus. The children will also learn that God sent Jesus to be our Savior.

ACTIVITY

A "Good News" Collage   Using old magazines, find and cut out pictures that show "good news." Arrange them on construction paper or poster board to make a collage. When it is finished, invite your child to tell about the good news in each picture.

WEEKLY PLANNER

On Sunday

Look around your church for artwork depicting angels. Then listen for references to angels in the Liturgy and in the hymns.

On the Web

blestarewe.com

Visit our Web site for the saint of the day and the reflection question of the week.

Saint of the Week

 Saint Joseph
(first century)

Joseph worked as a carpenter in Nazareth. He was chosen by God to be the husband of Mary and the foster father of Jesus. We know from the early events in Jesus' life that Joseph obeyed and trusted God and took good care of Jesus and Mary.

Patron Saint of: fathers and carpenters
Feast Days: March 19, May 1

A Prayer for the Week

Loving God, we are glad that you chose Joseph to care for Jesus and Mary. Help the members of our family love and care for one another as Jesus, Mary, and Joseph did. Amen.

Take Home

✝ Scripture Background

Before the Time of Jesus

Angels   Angels are spiritual beings with intelligence and free will, created by God to serve him and to act as messengers to carry out the plan of Salvation. In the Old Testament, God on occasion directly communicated with his people. However, over time, angels more commonly served as God's messengers. They also watched over God's people, and were sometimes instruments of God's justice. You can read about an angel announcing the birth of John the Baptist in Luke 1:11–20 and about the Angel Gabriel's visit to Mary in Luke 1:26–38.

OUR CATHOLIC TRADITION   in Art

The Annunciation   The Annunciation is one of the most frequently depicted Scripture stories by famous "old master" artists. One of the greatest is by the Italian Renaissance master Fra Angelico, a Dominican friar. In 1439 he was commissioned to paint religious pictures, known as frescoes, on the walls of the friars' rooms in the friary of San Marco in Florence, Italy. The Annunciation, however, he reserved for a very special place at the top of a staircase. The painting can still be seen in that same spot, just as it was hundreds of years ago.

9 Jesus Is God's Son

LET US PRAY We praise you, O God.
Your love for us is wonderful.

Based on Psalm 136:1–4

Share

Good news makes people happy.
Look at each picture.
Tell the good news that you
think each person hears.

Draw yourself hearing good news.

What good
news did
God send?

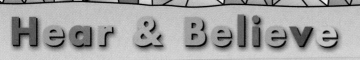

Hear & Believe

✝ Scripture The Good News

A long time ago, God sent the Angel Gabriel to Mary. Gabriel had good news for Mary. He told Mary that God wanted her to be the mother of a special baby. God wanted her to name the baby Jesus. This special baby would be the Son of God. Mary said, "Yes, I will do whatever God wants."

Based on Luke 1:26–38

Mary Said Yes

Mary was a young Jewish woman who lived in Nazareth. She was good and holy. Mary listened to the **Angel** Gabriel's message. Mary said yes to God. She would be the mother of God's Son. Gabriel told Mary that God would watch over her. Mary trusted God.

Activity Color the letters. Read the words the Angel Gabriel said to Mary.

HAIL MARY, FULL OF GRACE

Why did God send his Son?

Hear & Believe

✝ Jesus Is Born

It was almost time for Mary's baby to be born. Mary and her husband Joseph had to travel to the town of Bethlehem. But there was no room for them in the inn. So Baby Jesus was born in a stable.

Based on Luke 2:1–7

? How do you think Mary and Joseph felt when Jesus was born?

Our Church Teaches

God loves us very much. God sent his own Son, **Jesus**, to be our **Savior**. The Son of God became one of us. He shared his life with us. He is always with us.

Activity Help Mary and her husband **Joseph** go from Nazareth to Bethlehem. Find the letters along the way. Write them in order on the lines below. The sentence will tell you about Jesus.

We Believe

God asked Mary to be the mother of his Son, Jesus. God sent Jesus to save us.

Faith Words
Savior
Jesus, the Son of God, is our Savior. He helps us and saves us.

Jesus is the __ __ __ __ __ __ __ __ .

How can we share the Good News about Jesus?

Respond

Telling the Good News

David likes his dad to read to him. He loves to hear Bible stories about Jesus. One day, David's dad read about the birth of Jesus.

Later that day, David went to play at his friend Mike's house. He told Mike the Good News about Jesus.

? What do you think David told his friend?

Activities

1. Learn to sign the words,
"I bring you good news."
Then share Good News about
Jesus with others.

| I | bring | you | good | news |

2. Color the spaces that have an X in them.
Whose name do you see?

How can we
celebrate the
Good News
about Jesus?

Prayer Celebration

A Good News Echo Prayer

Did you ever hear an echo?
You can pray an echo prayer.
Just repeat the words you hear.

Leader: Jesus, we believe you are the Son of God.

All: Jesus, we believe you are the Son of God.

Leader: Jesus, we believe you are always with us.

All: Jesus, we believe you are always with us.

Leader: Jesus, we believe you love us very much.

All: Jesus, we believe you love us very much.

Ⓐ Draw a line to connect the parts of each sentence.

1. An angel is a ● ● own Son.

2. Jesus' mother is ● ● our Savior.

3. Jesus is God's ● ● Mary.

4. God sent Jesus to be ● ● messenger from God.

Ⓑ Write or draw something that you can tell others about the Good News of Jesus' birth.

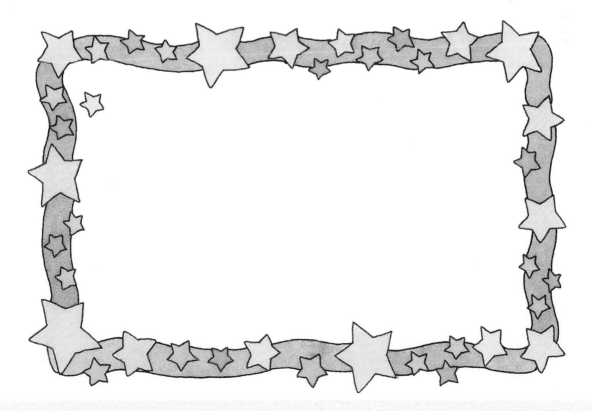

9 Chapter Review

C **Circle** the words that complete the sentences.

1. Mary grew up in the town of ____.
   Bethlehem   **Nazareth**

2. The Angel Gabriel had ____ for Mary.
   sad news   **good news**

3. Mary said ____ to God.
   no   **yes**

4. The husband of Mary was ____.
   Joseph   **John**

5. Jesus was born in the town of ____.
   Nazareth   **Bethlehem**

D **Write** the missing words to this echo prayer.

_____
- -
Jesus, you are the _____.
_____
- - - - - - - - - - - - - - -
_____, you are the Son of God.

Take Home

FAMILY TIME

We Celebrate the Gift of Eucharist

In this chapter, the children will come to recognize that the words of the Eucharistic Prayer at Mass describe the Last Supper that Jesus shared with his disciples on the night before he died. They will learn that Jesus is present in the Eucharist as a sign of God's love for us. During the prayer celebration, the children will genuflect and bow as signs of respect for the Blessed Sacrament.

ACTIVITY

A Family Celebration Check your calendar to see when your next family celebration will be. Plan together for the event. Who will be invited? How will you decorate? What special foods will you have? Will you need help from family and friends?

WEEKLY PLANNER

On Sunday

Before Mass, make a visit to the tabernacle. Demonstrate how we genuflect and bow to show respect for the Blessed Sacrament.

On the Web

blestarewe.com

 Visit our Web site for the saint of the day and the reflection question of the week.

Saint of the Week

 Saint Katharine Drexel
(1858–1955)

Katharine Drexel founded the Sisters of the Blessed Sacrament. Their mission includes spreading the Gospel and teaching about the Eucharist. Katharine used her wealth to establish missions and schools for Native and African Americans. She was canonized, or declared a saint, in 2000 by Pope John Paul II.

Feast Day: March 3

A Prayer for the Week

Loving God, give us thankful hearts to celebrate the gift of your Son in the Eucharist. Help us share with others our belief that Jesus Christ is truly present in the Blessed Sacrament. Amen.

Take Home

FAMILY TIME

✝ Scripture Background

In the Time of Jesus

Passover Meal The Jewish Passover meal commemorates the freeing of the Israelites from Egypt (Exodus 12). Passover was and still is the Jewish festival of freedom and redemption. By remembering God's saving acts, it gave people in Jesus' time hope in the face of oppression. Jesus' Last Supper was a Passover meal, which took on new meaning when he died and rose from the dead to save us from sin and enable us to have eternal life. You can read accounts of Jesus' last Passover meal, the Last Supper, in Matthew 26:17–30, Mark 14:12–26, and Luke 22:7–20.

OUR CATHOLIC TRADITION in Worship

Tabernacles The word *tabernacle* means "tent," or "dwelling place." The word is used in the Bible to describe the special tent in which the Ark of the Covenant with the tablets of the law was kept while the Hebrew people were in the desert. When Solomon built the Temple in Jerusalem, the Ark was housed in the Holy of Holies. The place of the ark was considered God's presence on earth.

In Catholic churches, the tabernacle is the place where the Eucharist is reserved so that it may be taken to homebound parishioners. Catholics pray before the tabernacle, remembering that Jesus Christ is present in the Blessed Sacrament.

King David bringing the Ark of the Covenant into Jerusalem, shown in an illuminated manuscript by an unknown fourteenth–century artist

10 We Celebrate the Gift of Eucharist

LET US PRAY

When you eat this bread and drink from this cup of wine, remember me.

Based on Luke 22:19–20

Share

Special meals can be fun.
There is good food.
There are people we like.

Plan a special meal for your family.
Circle the foods you want at this meal.

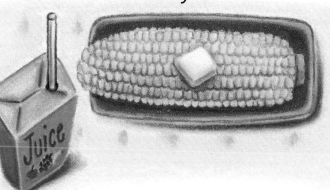

Draw another food you would
like to eat at this meal.

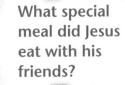

What special meal did Jesus eat with his friends?

Hear & Believe

🕯 Worship A Special Meal

On the night before he died, Jesus ate a special meal with his friends. We call this meal the Last Supper. Here is what Jesus said and did.

Jesus took bread from the table. He gave God thanks and praise. Then he broke the bread. He gave it to his friends and said, "Take this bread and eat it. This is my Body."

When supper was ended, Jesus took a cup of wine. He thanked God. He gave the cup to his friends and said, "Take this and drink from it. This is the cup of my Blood."

Based on Eucharistic Prayer I for Children

Jesus Is with Us

At the **Last Supper**, Jesus shared the gift of himself with his friends. Today Jesus comes to us in a holy meal called the **Eucharist**. We celebrate the Eucharist with our parish community at Mass. We remember all that Jesus did and said at the Last Supper on the night before he died. We thank God for the gift of Jesus' Body and Blood.

Activity Complete the sentence.
The holy meal that Jesus shares with us at Mass is called the

_____

- -

_____ .

Faith Words

Last Supper
The Last Supper is the holy meal that Jesus shared with his friends on the night before he died.

Eucharist
The Eucharist is the holy meal that Jesus shares with us at Mass. The bread and wine become the Body and Blood of Jesus.

How can we show our love for Christ in the Eucharist?

Hear & Believe

Showing Love for Jesus

One Friday morning, Miss Dooling's class visited the parish church. She showed the children the **tabernacle**. She reminded them that Jesus is present. So they all knelt down to pray. They made the Sign of the Cross. Then they prayed quietly with their hearts.

Mr. Lee walked up to the tabernacle. He opened the door with a key. Miss Dooling said that Mr. Lee brings Holy Communion to people who cannot come to Mass. This way they, too, get to share in Jesus' holy meal.

? How does Mr. Lee show his love for Jesus?

Activities

1. These objects help us remember Jesus.

Connect the dots. What do you see?

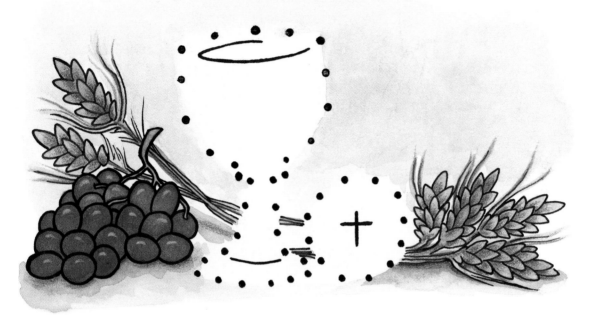

2. Do you remember what Jesus said
at the Last Supper? Finish the sentences.

Take this bread and eat it.
This is my

_____

- -

_____.

Take this and drink from it.
This is the cup of my

_____

- -

_____.

How can
we pray before
the Blessed
Sacrament?

Prayer Celebration

A Prayer of Adoration

We **adore** Jesus Christ by kneeling or bowing before the Blessed Sacrament.

Leader: Come let us adore the Lord, and bow down in worship. (*All bow.*)

All: Lord, we **adore you.** (*All rise.*)

Leader: Let us kneel before the Lord on the left knee. (*All kneel.*)

All: Lord, we **adore you.** (*All stand.*)

Leader: Let us kneel before the Lord on the right knee. (*All kneel.*)

All: Lord, we **adore you.** (*All stand.*)

Leader: Let us kneel before the Lord on both knees. (*All kneel.*)

All: Lord, we **adore you.** (*All stand.*)

Based on Psalm 95:6–7 and the Maronite Rite of Kneeling

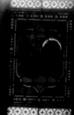

A **Complete** the sentences with words from the box.

tabernacle

Jesus

Eucharist

1. The holy meal that Jesus shares with us at Mass is called the _____ _____ .

2. _____ is present in the Eucharist.

3. The Eucharist is kept in a special container _____ called a _____ .

B **Draw or write** about how you can adore Jesus in the Blessed Sacrament.

C **Draw a line** to connect the parts of each sentence.

1. At the Last Supper
Jesus gave us the ● ● "This is the
cup of my Blood."

2. Jesus took the
bread and said, ● ● "This is my Body."

3. Jesus took the cup
of wine and said, ● ● Eucharist.

4. Another name for
the Eucharist is ● ● the Blessed
Sacrament.

D **Draw or write** about how Saint Katharine
Drexel showed her love for Jesus.

Take Home

FAMILY TIME

Jesus Teaches Us About Forgiveness

In this chapter, the children will hear the Bible story about Zacchaeus, a tax collector. They will learn that God's laws help them make good choices. The children will come to understand the importance of saying they are sorry when they have chosen to do wrong. They will learn that God is always ready to forgive them.

ACTIVITY

Read All About It   Read *Where the Wild Things Are* by Maurice Sendak (HarperCollins) with your child. Discuss the ending of the book as to how it relates to forgiveness and reconciliation.

WEEKLY PLANNER

On Sunday

Spend a few moments before Mass thinking about how you failed to be loving people. Reverently pray "Lord, have mercy."

On the Web

blestarewe.com

Visit our Web site for the saint of the day and the reflection question of the week.

Saint of the Week

Saint John Vianney (1786–1859)

John Vianney was ordained a priest after the French Revolution. He was sent to a poor parish in Ars, where Catholics were lax about their faith. Father Vianney prayed for them and visited every family. He spent hours hearing confessions. Because of his understanding and holiness, people came back to church.

Feast Day: August 4

A Prayer for the Week

Loving God, you are always ready to forgive us when we choose to do wrong. Help our family to be loving and forgiving in the days ahead. Amen.

Take Home

FAMILY TIME

✝ Scripture Background

In the Time of Jesus

Tax Collectors   In the time of Jesus, tax collectors were hated because they worked for the Romans, who were the occupiers of Palestine. Often, tax collectors overcharged their own people and could call upon Roman authority to punish those unwilling to pay the excessive rates. When Jesus goes to the homes of the tax collectors Matthew and Zacchaeus, he is accused of eating with sinners. Jesus replied that he did not come to call the righteous, but sinners. He even calls Matthew to be one of his Apostles.

You can read about Matthew and Zacchaeus in Matthew 9:9–13 and Luke 19:1–10.

OUR CATHOLIC TRADITION in Bible Times

Sycamore Trees   The Gospel story about Zacchaeus tells how he climbed up a sycamore tree to see Jesus over a crowd of people. The view from the sycamore tree enabled Zacchaeus, a short man, to see Jesus clearly.

Jericho, where the story takes place, is agriculturally rich and full of tree groves. The sycamore is a type of fig tree, called the mulberry fig, with edible fruit. This tree is not the same as the American sycamore. Zacchaeus found the Jericho sycamore tree convenient for climbing because of its low, spreading branches. Today, many families in Jericho still eat the figs from the sycamore tree.

11 Jesus Teaches Us about Forgiveness

Forgive me, O God, for I have done wrong.

Based on Luke 18:13

Share

Sometimes we do what is right.

Sometimes we do what is wrong.

Look at these pictures.

Draw a 🙂 if the action is right.

Draw a ☹ if the action is wrong.

What does Jesus teach us to do?

Hear & Believe

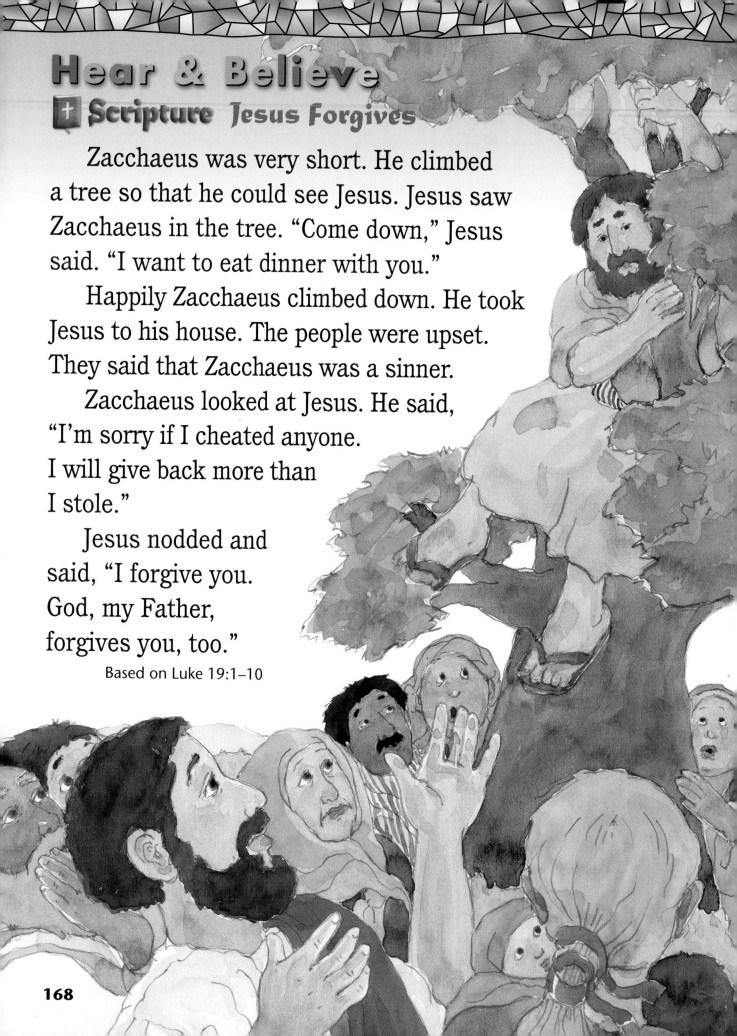

Zacchaeus was very short. He climbed a tree so that he could see Jesus. Jesus saw Zacchaeus in the tree. "Come down," Jesus said. "I want to eat dinner with you."

Happily Zacchaeus climbed down. He took Jesus to his house. The people were upset. They said that Zacchaeus was a sinner.

Zacchaeus looked at Jesus. He said, "I'm sorry if I cheated anyone. I will give back more than I stole."

Jesus nodded and said, "I forgive you. God, my Father, forgives you, too."

Based on Luke 19:1–10

168

What Jesus Wants

Zacchaeus was a selfish man. But he was sorry and began to help others. Jesus loved Zacchaeus and forgave him. Jesus teaches us to love God and others. When we do not act in a loving way, God wants us to be sorry. God will always **forgive** us.

Activity Draw a picture of Jesus and Zacchaeus eating dinner.

Faith Words
forgive
The word *forgive* means "to excuse or pardon".

How does God want us to act?

Hear & Believe

✝ The Golden Rule

One day, Jesus saw a great crowd of people following him. He went up a mountain, sat down, and began to teach his followers.

Jesus said, "Do to other people what you would want them to do to you. This is the law of God."

Based on Matthew 5:1–2, 7:12

? How do you want other people to treat you?

Our Church Teaches

Jesus wants us to obey God's laws. The laws of God help us choose to do what is right. When we choose to do what is wrong, we **sin**. When we sin, we turn away from God. Sin also hurts our friendship with other people. But God never stops loving us. He is always ready to forgive us.

Activity We show love for others with the words we say to them. Circle the words that show love for others. Write other loving words in the word balloon.

Faith Words

sin
To sin is to choose to do something that we know is wrong.

"Thank you."

"I don't like you."

"Let's be friends."

"I'm sorry."

"Don't play with her."

"Can I help you?"

How can we forgive someone?

Respond

A Forgiveness Story

Ricky played his video game over and over again. His mom told him to stop. She told Ricky to do his homework. Ricky was angry and said something mean to his mom. So she sent him to his room.

Ricky lay on his bed. He heard his parents talking. He heard his little sisters playing. He wanted to be with them. But soon Ricky fell asleep.

When Ricky awoke, he saw a bowl of hot soup on his table. Next to the soup was a note from his mom.

? What do you think the note said?

To ~ Ricky

Activities

1. Write the answers on the lines.

If you hurt someone, what can you say?

_____

- -

_____.

Someone is sorry for hurting you. What can you say?

_____

- -

_____.

2. Color the spaces marked with a † green.

Color the other spaces as you like.

What words do you see?

How can we celebrate God's forgiveness?

173

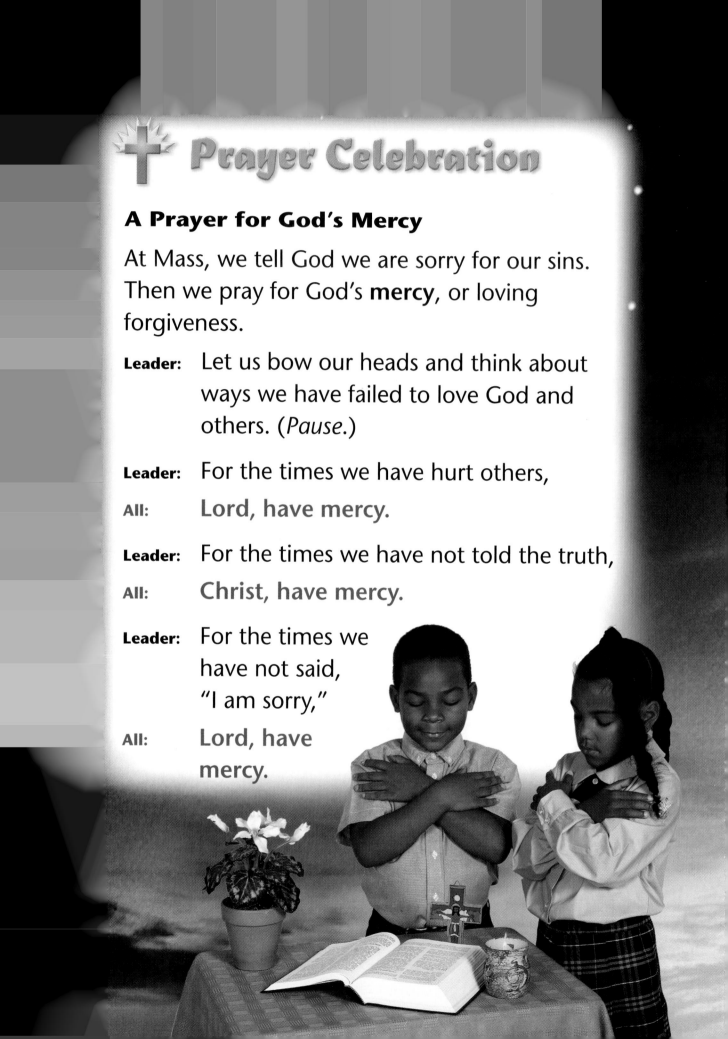

✞ Prayer Celebration

A Prayer for God's Mercy

At Mass, we tell God we are sorry for our sins. Then we pray for God's **mercy**, or loving forgiveness.

Leader: Let us bow our heads and think about ways we have failed to love God and others. (*Pause.*)

Leader: For the times we have hurt others,

All: Lord, have mercy.

Leader: For the times we have not told the truth,

All: Christ, have mercy.

Leader: For the times we have not said, "I am sorry,"

All: Lord, have mercy.

A **Circle** "yes" if the action is right.
Circle "no" if the action is wrong.

1. Judy plays fair.   **yes   no**

2. Someone calls Ellen names.   **yes   no**

3. Andy makes peace with Joey.   **yes   no**

4. Someone hits you.   **yes   no**

B **Draw a line** to match each picture
to the words of a child.

1.    •   • "I'm sorry, Mom."

2.    •   • "I forgive you."

3.    •   • "Lord, have mercy."

C **Complete** each sentence with a word from the box.

wrong	laws	sorry	forgive

_____

1. Jesus wants us to obey God's _____.

2. Sin is choosing to do what we know is

_____

_____

_____

3. Zacchaeus was _____ and began to help others.

_____

4. God is always ready to _____ us.

D **Write** the words of "The Golden Rule."

_____

_____

_____

_____

Take Home

FAMILY TIME

We Pray with God's Word

In this chapter, the children will discover how and where Jesus prayed. They will experience using their imagination to pray with the Gospel story of Jesus blessing the children. By putting themselves into the story, they will imagine what they would see, hear, feel, say, and do. The children will learn that praying with Bible stories can help them grow closer to Jesus.

ACTIVITY

Just Relax! The first step in praying with a Gospel story is to relax. Practice with your child. Sit comfortably in a quiet place. Close your eyes. Then breathe slowly while concentrating on your breathing. If you become distracted, bring your attention back to your breathing.

WEEKLY PLANNER

On Sunday

Listen carefully to the Gospel story during Mass. Imagine what it would be like to be in the story.

On the Web

blestarewe.com

Visit our Web site for the saint of the day and the reflection question of the week.

Saint of the Week

Saint Mark
(first century)

Mark was a member of the early Church in Jerusalem. He traveled with Paul and Barnabas on their first missionary journey. Mark's Gospel was the first to be written. It shows us the humanity of Jesus and challenges us to see how our lives connect to Jesus' suffering, Death, and Resurrection.

Feast Day: April 25

A Prayer for the Week

Dear Lord, bless our family with your presence. Help us hear your voice as we pray with Gospel stories. Help us live out the lessons we learn from your holy Word. Amen.

Take Home

FAMILY TIME

✝ Scripture Background

In the Time of Jesus

Children Jesus blesses the children and tells his listeners that they must be like little children to enter the Kingdom of Heaven. The chief characteristic of children is acceptance; they know best how to accept gifts—with openness and faith. Jesus says that only those who accept the Kingdom of God as a gift received through faith may enter it. Jesus goes against the common judgment of children in his day—that they hold no legal rights—by stating the special relationship they have with him. You can read about Jesus blessing the children in Mark 10:10–16.

OUR CATHOLIC TRADITION in Prayer

The Spiritual Exercises Ignatius of Loyola, born in Spain in 1491, became the founder of the Society of Jesus, or Jesuits. While studying his own spiritual life, Ignatius took notes on his experiences with prayer, suffering, and conversion of heart. His writings became known as the *Spiritual Exercises.* The exercises include Ignatius's approach to meditation. His method involves asking God for a special grace, reflecting on a Gospel scene by using one's imagination and senses, putting oneself into the scene, and applying the Gospel message to one's own life. Ignatius believed that everyone could learn to pray in this way. The *Spiritual Exercises* became Ignatius's greatest single contribution to Western spirituality.

12 We Pray with God's Word

Based on Luke 11:1

Share

People pray in many ways. Think about how you pray. How do you talk to and listen to God?

Mark an X in each picture that shows how you pray.

Circle your favorite way to pray.

How did Jesus pray?

Hear & Believe

✝ Scripture The Prayer of Jesus

The Bible tells us how and where Jesus prayed. He prayed with his heart and his voice. He prayed with his mind.

Jesus prayed with his family in the **Temple**. Jesus prayed alone in the desert. Sometimes he prayed on a mountain. Sometimes he prayed in a boat.

After the Last Supper, Jesus sang the **Psalms** with his friends. Then he went into a garden to pray.

The Temple in Jerusalem

Luke 2:41–52

A Bible land desert

Luke 4:1

A Bible land mountain

Matthew 14:23

180

Praying Like Jesus

We can learn to pray like Jesus.
We can pray aloud with our voices.
We can pray silently with our hearts
and minds. We can pray alone or with
other people. We can pray anywhere
and anytime.

Activity Draw a picture of your favorite place to pray.

The Sea of Galilee
Matthew 14:13

The Garden of Gethsemane
Matthew 26:30

How can we grow closer to Jesus?

Hear & Believe

Prayer Time

Sister Margaret said, "Children, it's prayer time. Paul, what Gospel story would you like us to pray with today?"

Paul answered, "I like the story about Jesus and the storm at sea."

"I like that one, too," said Betsy.

"That's a good story to pray with," said Sister Margaret. "So, let's close our eyes and be very quiet. Picture Jesus and his friends in the boat. Jesus is tired and falls asleep. Suddenly, a storm comes. The wind blows. Big waves start to fill the boat with water. Jesus' friends are afraid."

Then Sister Margaret said, "Imagine that you are in the boat with Jesus. How do you feel when the storm comes? What do you say to Jesus? What does Jesus do?"

? How do you think the children answered the questions?

Our Church Teaches

We can pray with **Gospel** stories from the Bible. There are four Gospels. They are the Good News of Jesus. They tell us how to show our love for God and other people. We grow closer to Jesus when we pray with the Gospels.

Activity Think about the times you are afraid. To find out what Jesus says to you, put the words on each sail in order. Then write the two sentences on the lines below.

not afraid Do be

YOU I with am

We Believe
Thinking about God's Word is a good way to pray. It helps us get closer to Jesus.

Faith Words
Gospel
The Gospel is the Good News of Jesus. There are four Gospels in the Bible.

_____

- -

_____.

_____

- -

_____.

How can we pray with a Gospel story?

Respond

Praying with God's Word

There are four steps in praying with a Gospel story.

Relax   Look and Listen   Imagine   Think

Relax Close your eyes. Become quiet. Ask God to fill your heart and mind.

Look and Listen Look at the picture of Jesus and the children. Listen to the Bible story.

✝ Jesus Blesses the Children

Jesus had been teaching all day. He was tired and sat down to rest.

Many parents started to bring their children to Jesus. They wanted Jesus to bless the children. But Jesus' friends told the people not to bother Jesus.

When Jesus saw this, he said, "Don't stop them. Let the children come closer. I love little children." Then Jesus placed his hands on the children. He gave them his blessing.

Based on Mark 10:10–16

Imagine Put yourself in the story. Imagine that your parents are taking you to see Jesus. He is on a hillside with his friends. Jesus is sitting under a tree.

Think Put yourself into the story. Ask yourself these questions.

Does Jesus see you?
Do you go up to him?
What do you say to Jesus?
What does Jesus say to you?

Activity
Draw yourself in the picture with Jesus and the children.

How else can we pray with a Gospel story?

Prayer Celebration

An Acting Prayer

You can pray by acting out a Bible story. Putting on a play helps you to think about the story. You can imagine what the people said and did.

Act out the story of Jesus blessing the children.

12 Chapter Review

A **Circle** the word that best completes each sentence.

1. Jesus prayed with his family in the _____.

   park   **Temple**

2. Jesus sang the _____ with his friends.

   Psalms   **Bible**

3. The Gospel is the Good News of _____.

   Moses   **Jesus**

4. The number of Gospels in the Bible is _____.

   six   **four**

B **Write or Draw** about how you like to pray.

C Think about the Gospel story, "Jesus Blesses the Children." **Write** the words that Jesus might have said to one of the children.

_____

- -

_____

- -

_____

- -

_____

- -

_____

Faith in Action

Shawl Ministry   Women in Holy Family Parish knit shawls for people who are sick or lonely. The knitters pray for the people who will get the shawls. Children in the parish school make cards to go with the shawls.

In Your Parish

Activity   How does your parish school show that it cares for people who are sick and lonely? Write a note to a sick or lonely person. Tell the person that you will pray for him or her.

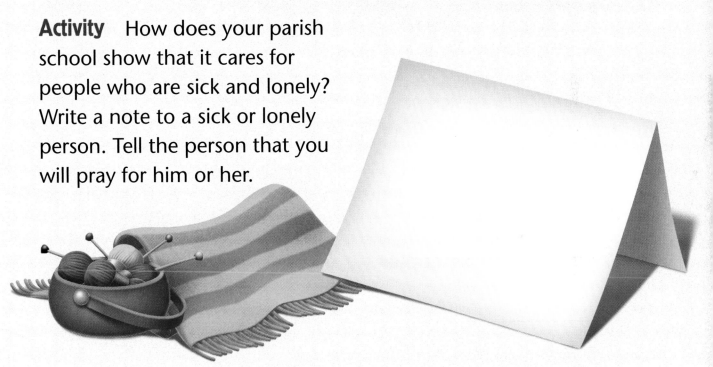

In Everyday Life

Activity   We can love and care for people in many ways. How can you show your love to someone in your family? What can you do to make a friend feel special?

Faith in Action

Special Helpers at Mass   Many people help the priest at Mass. Some helpers give out Holy Communion. One helper says, "The Body of Christ." We say, "Amen." Another helper says, "The Blood of Christ." We say, "Amen." These helpers are called extraordinary ministers of Holy Communion.

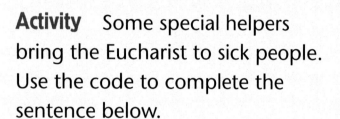

In Your Parish

Activity   Some special helpers bring the Eucharist to sick people. Use the code to complete the sentence below.

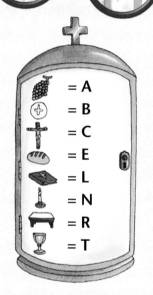

= A
= B
= C
= E
= L
= N
= R
= T

The Eucharist for sick people is kept in the

___ ___ ___ ___ ___ ___ ___ ___

___ ___ ___ ___ ___ ___ ___ ___ ___ .

In Everyday Life

Activity   Think about the meals you share with your family. How can you help make your family mealtime special?

Faith in Action

Secretary and Custodian Each parish school has workers who do important jobs. The secretary answers the phone, types letters to parents, and keeps all kinds of lists up to date. The custodian cleans the school and makes sure the lights, heat, and refrigerator work. All workers should be respected and treated fairly.

In Your Parish

Activity Who are some of the workers in your parish school? What jobs do they do? How can your parish show respect for its school workers?

In Everyday Life

Activity People work to get the things they need for themselves and for their families.
People need food, water, a house, clothes, books, and a doctor's care.

Find and circle pictures of these needs.

Faith in Action

Praying with Scripture   Each week in many parishes, small groups gather to pray. They read the Scripture readings for the next Sunday's Mass. They think about the readings. They share their thoughts. Then they pray about how they can show their love for God and others.

In Your Parish

Activity   Think of questions to ask a prayer group in the parish. Plan to tell how you pray with a Gospel story.

In Everyday Life

Activity   Choose and circle one of the places where Jesus prayed.

desert   mountain

garden   boat

Draw a picture of yourself praying with Jesus in that place.

Read the names of the chapters.

Think about the pictures.

Draw a line to show what you learned in each chapter.

1. Jesus Is God's Son ●

2. We Celebrate the Gift of Eucharist ●

3. Jesus Teaches Us About Forgiveness ●

4. We Pray with God's Word ●

A **Complete** the sentences with words from the box.

| sin   Eucharist   Gospels   Last Supper   Savior |

1. Jesus is the Son of God and our

   _____

   -

   _____.

2. The meal that Jesus shared with his friends on the night before he died is called the

   _____

   -

   _____.

3. The holy meal that Jesus shares with us at

   _____

   -

   Mass is the _____.

4. When we choose to do something that

   _____

   -

   we know is wrong, we _____.

5. The Good News about Jesus is in the

   _____

   -

   four _____.

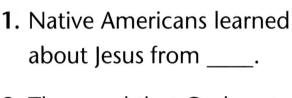

Unit Review

B **Draw** a line to the name that completes each sentence.

1. Native Americans learned about Jesus from ____.

  ●   ● Mary

2. The angel that God sent with good news for Mary was ____.

  ●   ● Katharine Drexel

3. The mother of God's Son Jesus is ____.

  ●   ● Joseph

4. The man who told Jesus that he was sorry if he cheated anyone was ____. ●

  ●   ● Gabriel

5. Mary's husband was ____.

  ●   ● Zacchaeus

C **Complete** each sentence by writing the letter of the missing word on the line.

1. Jesus prayed with his family in the ____.

2. After Mass the Eucharist is kept in the ____.

3. God's loving forgiveness is called ____.

4. Jesus wants us to obey ____.

5. We can ____ anywhere and anytime.

A. God's laws

B. mercy

C. pray

D. Temple

E. tabernacle

D **Draw** yourself praying with a Gospel story.

The Holy Spirit

Jesus sends us the Holy Spirit to help us live as Jesus' followers. Sometimes it is hard to know what God wants us to do. We can pray to the Holy Spirit for help.

Let us follow the Holy Spirit.
Based on Galatians 5:25

Paul sailed to different cities in a boat like this one. He taught people that the Holy Spirit is our helper. When we love others the Holy Spirit helps us to be kind.

If You Believe and I Believe

Traditional from Zimbabwe
Adaptation of English traditional as taught by Tarasai
Arranged by John L. Bell

If you be-lieve— and I be-lieve And we to-geth-er pray,——

The Ho-ly Spir-it must come down And set God's peo-ple free,——

And set God's peo-ple free,—— And set God's peo-ple free;——

The Ho-ly Spir-it must come down And

set God's peo-ple free.——

Take Home

FAMILY TIME

Jesus Promises the Holy Spirit

In this chapter, the children will read about Jesus' promise to send the Holy Spirit. They will learn that the Holy Spirit is the gift of God's love. They will discover that the Holy Spirit helps us remember Jesus' teachings. Together they will praise God the Father, Son, and Holy Spirit.

ACTIVITY

A Welcome Sign Showing a spirit of hospitality is one way to share love with others. Invite a family from your parish or neighborhood to your home for dinner or dessert. In preparation, discuss with your child the importance of hospitality, and together make a welcome sign for the family you invite.

Welcome to our home.

WEEKLY PLANNER

On Sunday
One image of the Holy Spirit is the dove. Look for images of the Holy Spirit while you are at church.

On the Web
blestarewe.com

Visit our Web site for the saint of the day and the reflection question of the week.

Saint of the Week
 Saint Dominic Savio (1842–1857)

Dominic Savio was born in Italy. At the time of his First Holy Communion, he considered Jesus and Mary to be his best friends. Dominic liked to pray and study, and was viewed as a peacemaker at his school. He became ill and died before his fifteenth birthday.

Patron Saint of: young boys
Feast Day: March 9

A Prayer for the Week

Come, Holy Spirit, fill our hearts with your gifts of love and peace. Help us follow the example of Saint Dominic Savio by being a sign of peace to everyone we meet. Amen.

Take Home

FAMILY TIME

✝ Scripture Background

In the Time of Jesus

The Advocate   In the Gospel of John 14:15–31, during the Last Supper discourses, Jesus makes a promise to his disciples. He says that after his departure, he will send another Advocate—himself being the first—to remain with them. Jesus specifies the conditions for receiving the Advocate as their love for him and the keeping of his commandments. This Advocate is clearly the Holy Spirit, the "Spirit of Truth," who after Jesus' Death and Resurrection will continue his work by helping the disciples understand the meaning of Jesus' teachings and deeds.

OUR CATHOLIC TRADITION in Symbols

The Dove   The image of the dove representing the Holy Spirit goes back to the origins of the Church, and the image of the dove in Scripture goes back to the story of Noah. As a sign of the union of the Holy Spirit and Jesus Christ, receptacles for the Eucharist that would be taken to the dying were made in the shape of a dove. The containers were hung above the altar in many churches since the early Middle Ages. They were originally made of precious metal, usually gold or silver. Later the dove was made of different materials, including gilded leather. The dove became the outer vessel holding the smaller container, or pyx, with the Blessed Sacrament inside.

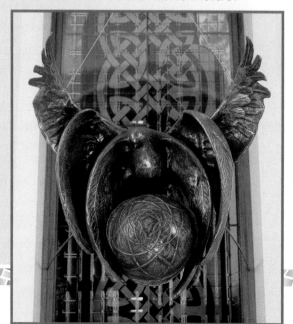

13 Jesus Promises the Holy Spirit

My Father will send you a helper to be with you always.

Based on John 14:16

Share

Your family loves you very much.
Your family helps you in many ways.
But your family needs helpers to
care for you and to help you learn.

Tell how each person helps you.

Write about a person who helps you.

_____

- -

_____

_____

- -

_____

Who is the
helper Jesus
asked his
Father to send?

Hear & Believe

The friends of Jesus were sad. They did not want Jesus to leave them. "Stay with us," they begged.

Jesus shook his head. "I must go away, but I will not leave you alone. I will ask God, my Father, to send you the Holy Spirit."

"Who is the Holy Spirit?" they asked.

"The Holy Spirit is the helper my Father will send to those who love me," Jesus said. "The Holy Spirit will teach you more about God's love. The Holy Spirit will help you remember all that I have told you."

Jesus' friends looked worried.

"Don't be afraid," Jesus said. "The Holy Spirit will bring you peace. He will always be with you."

Based on John 14:15–31

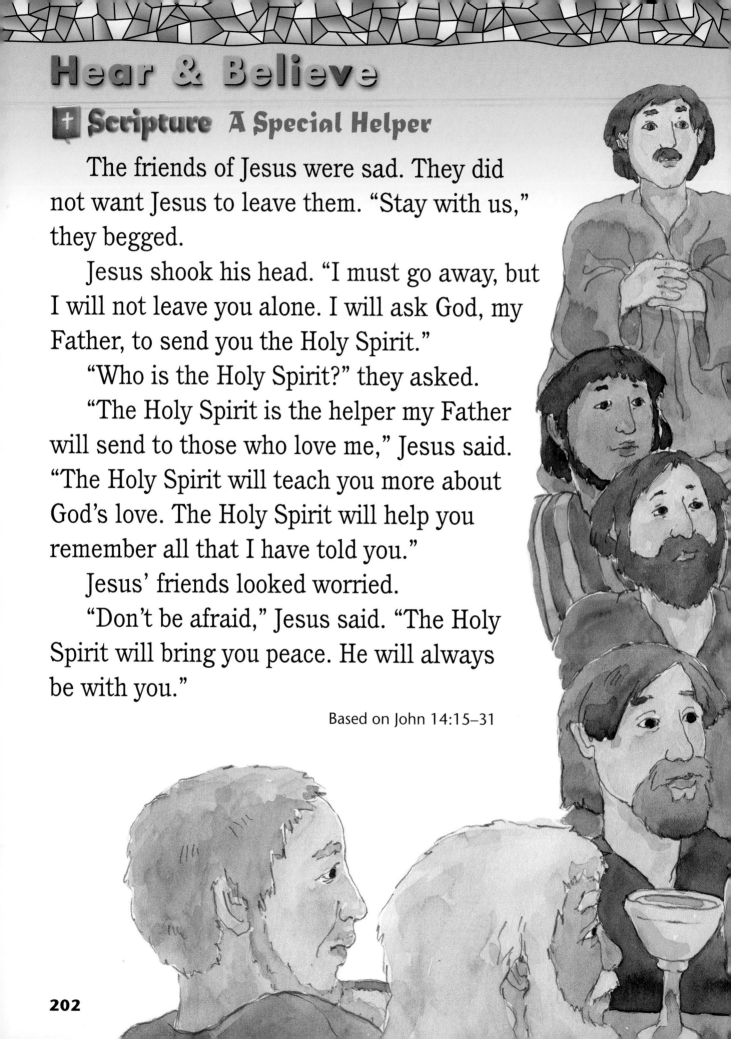

Our Church Teaches

God the Holy Spirit is the gift of God's love to us. The Holy Spirit is always with us. He helps us and guides us.

Activity Think about times when the Holy Spirit could help you. Draw a picture about one of these times.

How else can the Holy Spirit help us?

Respond

Terry's Problem

One morning, Terry was waiting for the school bus. Something very scary happened. Two older boys pushed a first grade boy into the street. The older boys thought it was funny. They began to laugh.

When Terry got to school, she told her teacher what happened. Terry was afraid that the other children might tease her.

That night, Terry's mother said, "You did the right thing. Your teacher will know how to handle the problem."

At bedtime, Terry's mother taught her this prayer. "Holy Spirit, help me always do what is right."

? Why did Terry's mother teach her this prayer?

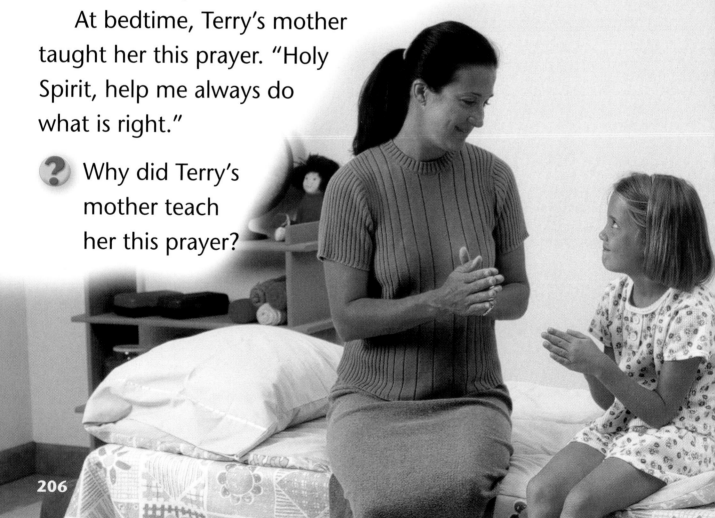

Activities

1. Color the border around the prayer. Then pray the prayer.

Holy Spirit, help me always do what is right.

2. Look at each picture. Circle the choice the Holy Spirit helps the children make.

to steal

to be honest

to make peace

to fight

How can we celebrate God's gift of the Holy Spirit?

Prayer Celebration

Glory Be to the Father

Let us now celebrate God's gift of the Holy Spirit by praising God with the prayer, "Glory Be to the Father."

Glory be to the Father
and to the Son
and to the Holy Spirit;
as it was in the beginning
is now, and ever shall be
world without end.

Amen.

Ⓐ Draw a line to connect the parts of each sentence.

1. Jesus promised
   to send •   • God's love.

2. The Holy Spirit
   helps us •   • the Holy Spirit.

3. The Holy Spirit
   is a gift of •   • with us.

4. The Holy Spirit
   is always •   • follow Jesus.

Ⓑ Circle the words that name choices
the Holy Spirit helps people make.

1. Susan will _____ at home.
   help   **be lazy**

2. José will _____ when he plays with his friends.
   cheat   **be fair**

3. Kim will _____ at Mass.
   play   **pray**

4. David will _____ at school.
   listen   **not listen**

C **Draw or write** about one way Saint Dominic Savio was a peacemaker.

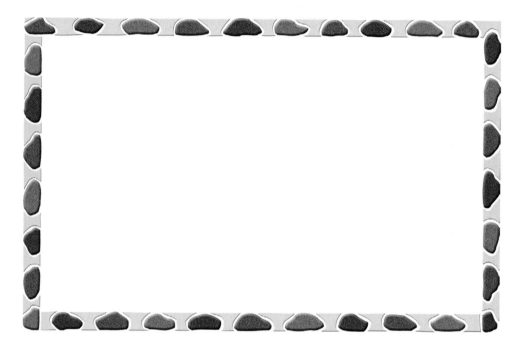

D **Write** the words that are missing from this part of the prayer.

_____

Glory be to the _____, and

_____

to the _____, and to the

_____ _____

_____ _____.

Take Home

FAMILY TIME

We Celebrate the Gift of the Holy Spirit

In this chapter, the children will learn that they receive God's gift of the Holy Spirit in the Sacraments. They will learn that the pouring of water in Baptism is a sign that all sin is washed away and that we are filled with God's love. The children will also learn that the oil used in Confirmation is a sign that the Holy Spirit is working in us to make our faith stronger.

ACTIVITY

Remembering Baptism Locate your child's baptismal certificate. Together, find the date and place of your child's Baptism. Talk about this special day. Plan a family celebration. If possible, invite your child's godparents.

WEEKLY PLANNER

On Sunday

Look at the baptismal font in your church. Remind your family that the Holy Spirit first came to them at Baptism.

On the Web

blestarewe.com

 Visit our Web site for the saint of the day and the reflection question of the week.

Saint of the Week

 Saint Turibius (1538–1606)

Turibius, a judge in Spain, was appointed archbishop of Lima, Peru, in 1580. He visited the villages in his territory, baptizing and confirming the people. Bishop Turibius built hospitals and became an advocate for the poor. He died during his last missionary journey.

Patron Saint of: Latin American bishops

Feast Day: March 23

A Prayer for the Week

Spirit of God, at our Baptism we were called to follow Jesus. Guide us as we try to follow the example of Saint Turibius. Help us spread the Good News and share our gifts with the poor. Amen.

Take Home

FAMILY TIME

† Scripture Background

In the Time of Jesus

Nicodemus Nicodemus was a Pharisee, a teacher, and a leader of the Jews. He appears in John's Gospel three times: questioning Jesus (John 3:1–21); defending Jesus (John 7:50–52); preparing Jesus' body for burial with Joseph of Arimathea (John 19:39). He seems to personify certain learned Jews who were well disposed toward Jesus, but did not adequately understand him, and had not reached the point of accepting him publicly. You may wish to read about Nicodemus questioning Jesus in John 3:1–21.

OUR CATHOLIC TRADITION in Rituals

Holy Oils Each year during Holy Week, there is a solemn ritual at the cathedral church. During the ritual, the holy oils used in the parishes throughout the coming year are blessed or consecrated by the bishop at the Chrism Mass. These oils are the Oil of Chrism, a mixture of olive oil and fragrant balm, used in Baptism, Confirmation, and Holy Orders; the Oil of Catechumens used to anoint adults preparing for Baptism; and the Oil of the Sick, used in the Sacrament of Anointing of the Sick. Parish representatives return to their churches with the holy oils, to be used in the celebration of Sacraments throughout the year.

St. Augustine's Cathedral in Tuscon, Arizona

14 We Celebrate the Gift of the Holy Spirit

O God, send your Holy Spirit to help and guide us.

Based on the Rite of Confirmation

Share

Water and oil are used in many ways. Circle the sign for water or oil under each picture.

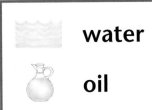

water

oil

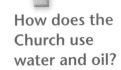

How does the Church use water and oil?

Hear & Believe

We receive the gift of the Holy Spirit in the **Sacraments**. Two of the Sacraments are Baptism and Confirmation.

In Baptism, the priest or deacon blesses water before he pours it on the person. He prays, "Father, by the power of the Holy Spirit, we ask you now to bless this water. May it wash away all sin and give us new life in Christ."

Based on the Rite of Baptism for Children

In Confirmation, the bishop uses holy oil to make the sign of the cross on the forehead of the person. He says, "Be sealed with the Gift of the Holy Spirit." This means "Be filled with God's Spirit."

Based on the Rite of Confirmation

214

The Holy Spirit Comes to Us

The Holy Spirit comes to us in the Sacraments. The Church celebrates the Sacraments as signs of God's love. In each Sacrament, the Holy Spirit gives us grace. This gift of grace helps us follow Jesus.

Faith Words

Sacraments
The Sacraments are special signs of God's love.

Activity Complete the sentences below with words from the box.

grace	**love**	**signs**

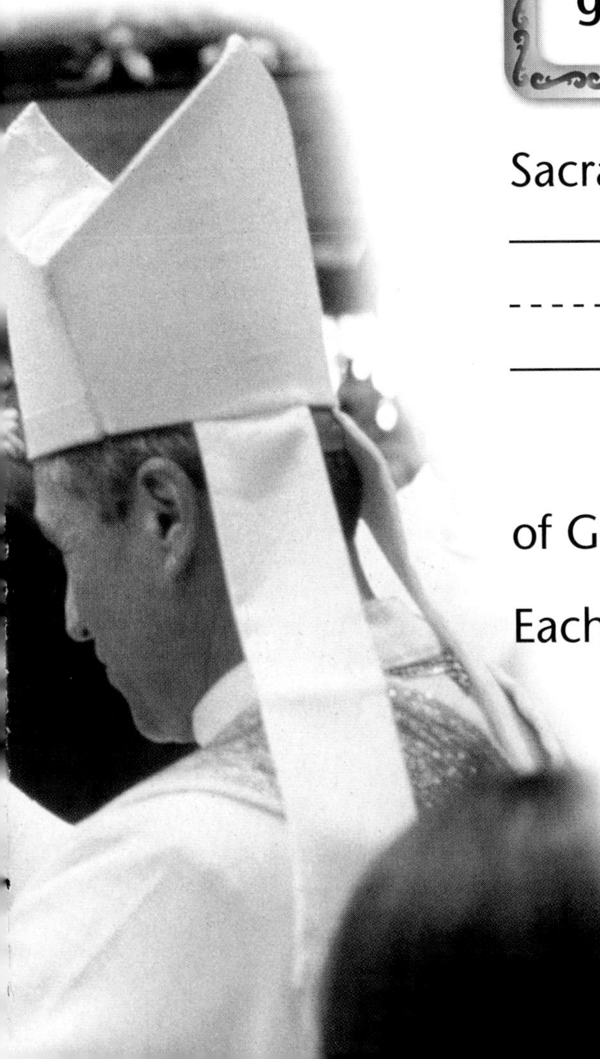

Sacraments are special

____

of God's ______________.

Each Sacrament gives us

______________________.

How else can the Holy Spirit help us?

Hear & Believe

How Mom Became a Catholic

We always went to Mass with Dad. Mom only came on special days like Christmas and Easter. She was not Catholic. She was Jewish.

I used to ask, "Why doesn't Mom become a Catholic?"

Dad always said, "Maybe someday she will."

Last year, my sister received her First Holy Communion. After that, Mom started to go to a special meeting at church. Dad said that she was learning about what Catholics believe.

Then on Holy Saturday night, we all went to church. During Mass, Mom and some other people received the Sacraments of Baptism, Confirmation, and the Eucharist. Mom became a member of the Catholic Church. She received the gift of the Holy Spirit.

? How do you think the Holy Spirit can help the child's mom?

Our Church Teaches

In the Sacrament of Baptism, we are washed clean of all sin. The water is a sign of new life. The Holy Spirit fills us with God's love. The Holy Spirit helps us live as good Catholics.

In the Sacrament of **Confirmation**, the Holy Spirit makes our faith in Jesus Christ stronger. The holy oil is a sign that the Holy Spirit is working in us.

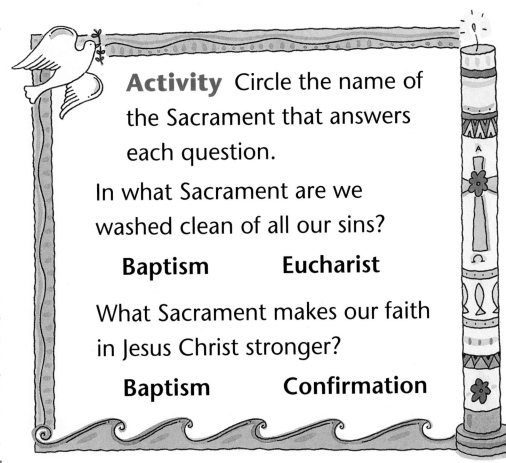

Activity Circle the name of the Sacrament that answers each question.

In what Sacrament are we washed clean of all our sins?

Baptism   **Eucharist**

What Sacrament makes our faith in Jesus Christ stronger?

Baptism   **Confirmation**

How can we show that the Holy Spirit lives in us?

217

Respond

✝ The Story of Nicodemus

One night, Nicodemus went secretly to Jesus. "What must I do to become a member of God's Kingdom?" he asked Jesus.

Jesus said, "You must be born of water and the Spirit."

"How can this happen?" Nicodemus asked.

Jesus explained, "If you believe in me, the Holy Spirit will bring you God's own life. This life will last forever."

"What is this life like?" Nicodemus asked.

Jesus explained, "Instead of living in darkness, you will live in the light. Instead of doing bad things, you will do what is good."

Based on John 3:1–21

❓ What do you think Nicodemus did next?

Activity

The Holy Spirit guides us to make good choices. Look at each picture. Read the sentences. Draw a line under the better choice.

Please take out the garbage.

Lisa watches TV.
Lisa takes out the garbage.

It's my turn to play.

Tim keeps playing with the truck.
Tim lets Bruce play with the truck.

Pray with us.

Rosa tries to sing and pray.
Rosa plays with her toys.

How can we pray to the Holy Spirit?

✝ Prayer Celebration

A Prayer to the Holy Spirit

Special prayers are said when holy oil is used in the Sacraments. We can pray with oil, too. The oil reminds us that the Holy Spirit is with us.

Leader: Let us call upon the Holy Spirit to help us follow Jesus.

All: Holy Spirit, help us and guide us.

Leader: (*Rub oil on each child's hands.*) The Holy Spirit lives in you. What is your prayer?

Child: Holy Spirit, help me and guide me.

A **Circle** the word that best completes each sentence.

1. We are washed clean of all sin in ____.
   Confirmation   **Baptism**

2. Special signs of God's love are called the ____.
   prayers   **Sacraments**

3. The sacrament that makes our faith stronger is ____.
   Confirmation   **Penance**

4. Jesus told Nicodemus that God's life lasts ____.
   forever   **ten years**

B **Write** the missing words that a bishop says at Confirmation when he blesses a person with holy oil.

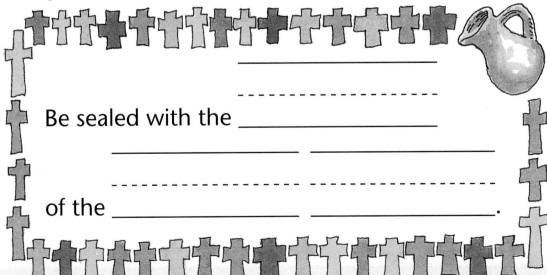

_____

Be sealed with the _____

_____ _____

of the _____ _____.

C **Draw a line** to the word that completes each sentence.

1. In each ____, the Holy Spirit ●   ● Catholics
gives us grace.

2. In Baptism, ____ is a sign ●   ● oil
of new life.

3. The Holy Spirit helps ●   ● Sacrament
us live as good ____.

4. In Confirmation, ____ is ●   ● water
a sign that the Holy Spirit
is working in us.

D **Draw or write** about a time when the
Holy Spirit helped you.

Take Home

FAMILY TIME

The Holy Spirit Is Our Helper

In this chapter, the children will come to understand that the Holy Spirit helps us follow Jesus. They will learn the Fruits of the Holy Spirit from Paul's letter to one of the early Christian communities. As the children use their good habits to show love for others, they will begin to realize that the Holy Spirit is acting in their lives.

ACTIVITY

Seeds of Virtue The family has been called the seedbed of virtue because it is in the family that children learn the good habits necessary for a Christian life. Purchase an envelope of seeds and make labels with the names of good habits you would like for your child. Together plant the seeds and watch them grow.

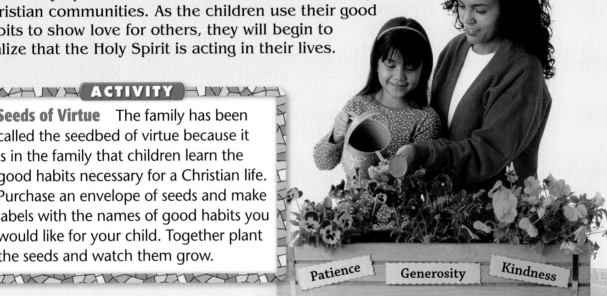

Patience   Generosity   Kindness

WEEKLY PLANNER

On Sunday

During the Prayer of the Faithful, ask the Holy Spirit to help you develop habits that will make you more loving.

On the Web

blestarewe.com

Visit our Web site for the saint of the day and the reflection question of the week.

Saint of the Week

 Saint Paul
(first century)

Paul, also known as Saul, was a devout Jew who had witnessed and condoned the martyrdom of Stephen. While on his way to arrest Christians, he heard the voice of Jesus. Paul experienced a conversion and spent the rest of his life teaching others about Jesus. Paul's letters to the early Christians are in the Bible.

Feast Day: January 25.

A Prayer for the Week

Loving God, you send us your Spirit to help us follow Jesus. You help us to be loving, gentle, and kind. We promise to use our good habits to help others. Amen.

Take Home

FAMILY TIME

✝ Scripture Background

In the Time of the Early Church

Letter to the Galatians   Paul wrote letters, or epistles, to some of the early Christian communities as well as to individual disciples. His letter to the Galatians, which includes the Fruits of the Holy Spirit, emphasizes the absolute importance of Christ and his cross as the way to Salvation and holiness. It stresses Christian freedom and perfecting the Mosaic Law. Whereas the Mosaic Law provided the Israelites with meticulous observance of ritual, social, and moral regulations; the new law presented a vision of the life of grace in Christ with the help of the Holy Spirit. You may wish to read all six chapters of Paul's letter.

Our Catholic Tradition in Theology

St. Thomas Aquinas   Thomas Aquinas, who lived in the thirteenth century, became known as one of the best thinkers in history. He greatly influenced theological thought in the Western Church. Aquinas developed a theology of the Holy Spirit based on his understanding of Isaiah 11:2–3 and Galatians 5:22–23. He taught not only that we should use the Holy Spirit's power and gifts in our lives, but that we should truly enjoy and feel close to the Holy Spirit, just as we do with a dear friend.

Aquinas believed that the Holy Spirit's peace and joy make us content and transform our hearts, changing fear and anxiety into security and the desire to give to others.

15 The Holy Spirit Is Our Helper

Let us follow the Holy Spirit.

Based on Galatians 5:25

Share

Some things we do are habits. Our habits can be good or bad. To brush our teeth every day is a good habit. To bite our nails is a bad habit.

Write a **G** in the box before Nick and Jenny's good habits. Write a **B** in the box before Nick and Jenny's bad habits.

☐ Jenny puts her toys away before bedtime.

☐ Nick always leaves his jacket on the floor.

☐ Nick says "thank you" when he gets a gift.

☐ Jenny prays to God each day.

☐ Jenny slams the door every morning.

How does the Holy Spirit help us learn good habits?

Hear & Believe

✝ Scripture A Letter from Paul

Paul became a follower of Jesus Christ. He wrote this letter to a group of the first **Christians**.

My Dear People,
Jesus Christ loves you. He wants you to love others the way you love yourselves. Sometimes it will be hard to be kind and helpful. But Christ gave you the Holy Spirit to be your helper and guide.
If you follow the Spirit, the **Fruits of the Holy Spirit** will be yours. You will act with love, joy, and peace. You will be patient, gentle, and kind. You will have self-control.

Based on Galatians 5:14–25

Kindness JOY Love

Our Church Teaches

When we practice good habits, we share the Fruits of the Holy Spirit with others. These Fruits are signs that the Holy Spirit is acting in our lives. When we do kind acts again and again, kindness becomes a habit. Our kindness teaches others about the kindness of God.

Activity Sara has a good habit. Cross out the letters **a** and **m** to find out what her good habit is. Then write the word to complete the sentence below.

amagmamemanamatmalamem

_____

- -

Sara is _____.

How can we use the Fruits of the Holy Spirit?

229

Respond

Tony's Saturday Habit

Tony is fun to play with. He shares his toys. He helps younger children learn new games. He stops fights by saying funny things. Everyone feels good when Tony is around. But Tony has a Saturday habit. He watches TV for three hours. All his friends want him to come out and play. But Tony says, "I can't. I need to watch my shows."

love

joy

? What do you think about Tony's habit?

Activities

1. Pick a Fruit of the Holy Spirit and circle it. Draw how you will use this Fruit with someone at home.

2. Pick another Fruit of the Holy Spirit and draw a box around it. Write about how you will use this Fruit in school.

How can we celebrate the Fruits of the Holy Spirit?

peace

patience

self-control

gentleness

kindness

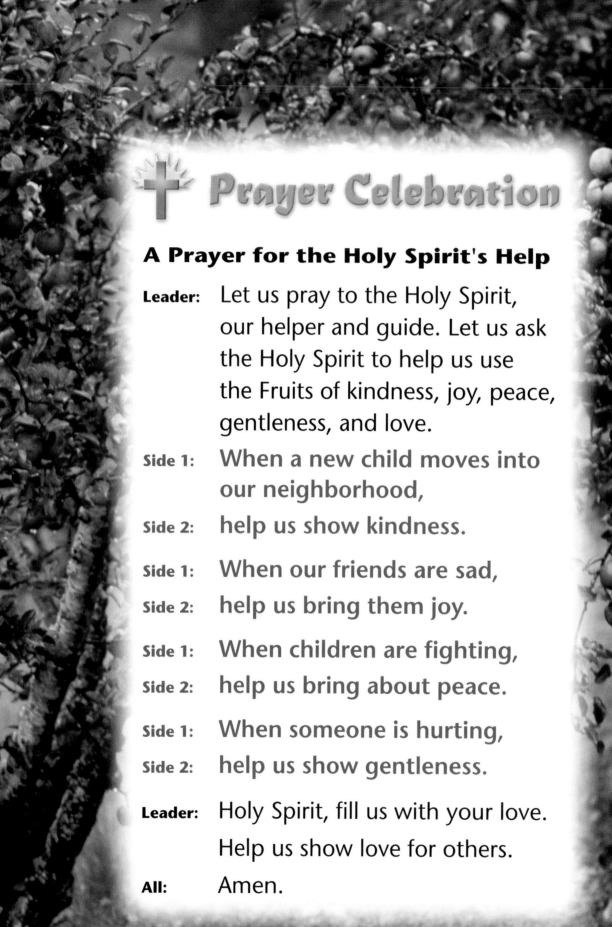

✝ Prayer Celebration

A Prayer for the Holy Spirit's Help

Leader: Let us pray to the Holy Spirit, our helper and guide. Let us ask the Holy Spirit to help us use the Fruits of kindness, joy, peace, gentleness, and love.

Side 1: When a new child moves into our neighborhood,

Side 2: help us show kindness.

Side 1: When our friends are sad,

Side 2: help us bring them joy.

Side 1: When children are fighting,

Side 2: help us bring about peace.

Side 1: When someone is hurting,

Side 2: help us show gentleness.

Leader: Holy Spirit, fill us with your love. Help us show love for others.

All: Amen.

A **Complete** the sentences with words from the box.

Fruits	Christians	joy
kind	Jesus Christ	

1. People who love and follow Jesus Christ

   _____

   are called _____ .

2. Paul's letter tells us that

   _____

   _____ loves us.

   _____

3. The _____ of the

   Holy Spirit are signs that he is acting
   in our lives.

4. The Holy Spirit helps us to be

   _____

   _____ to others.

5. The Holy Spirit helps us share our love

   _____

   and _____ with others.

B **Circle** the words that name Fruits of the Holy Spirit.

joy	light	peace	hate
quiet	gentleness	sadness	self-control
patience	fear	kindness	love

C **Write** one thing that Saint Thomas Aquinas taught people about the Holy Spirit.

Take Home

FAMILY TIME

The Holy Spirit Helps Us Pray

In this chapter, the children will read some of Jesus' teachings about prayer that are in the Bible. They will learn that the Holy Spirit teaches us how to pray for the things we need. Each child will write a prayer of petition to the Holy Spirit, and will participate in a Holy Spirit prayer celebration.

ACTIVITY

A Prayer Box   Decorate a small empty box with symbols of the Holy Spirit, such as doves and flames of fire. Leave blank pieces of paper next to the box. Invite your family to write petitions on the papers and to place them in the prayer box. Together, read the petitions and pray for each other's requests.

WEEKLY PLANNER

On Sunday

During Mass, listen to the readings and prayers for times when the Holy Spirit is mentioned. On your way home, discuss some of these times.

On the Web

blestarewe.com

Visit our Web site for the saint of the day and the reflection question of the week.

Saint of the Week

Saint Clare (1193–1253)

Clare, a friend and follower of Francis of Assisi, came from a wealthy Italian family in Assisi. She joined Francis in living a life of poverty and simplicity. Francis helped Clare found a religious community of women known as the Poor Clares. The nuns live a contemplative life of work and prayer. Their mission is to pray for the world and for the Church.

Feast Day: August 11.

A Prayer for the Week

Come Holy Spirit, fill our family with your love. Help us place our trust in Jesus and show our love for others as Saint Clare did. Amen.

Take Home

FAMILY TIME

✠ Scripture Background

In the Time of Jesus

The Prayer of Petition   Requests made to God are called prayers of petition. Jesus speaks of praying for one's needs and for the healing of the sick. He speaks of praying for ourselves and for others. Within the prayer of petition, however, is the understanding that while these prayers are offered to God in faith and expectation, through Christ and the Holy Spirit, God's responses are based on his will and what is best for the Kingdom. Some of Jesus' teachings about prayers of petition can be found in Matthew 6:5–15; 7:7–11.

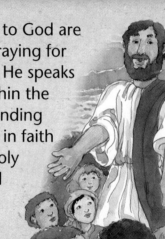

OUR CATHOLIC TRADITION in Liturgy

The Holy Spirit's Role in Liturgy   Prayers to the Holy Spirit reveal the Spirit's role in the liturgical life of the Church. During the Eucharistic Prayer at Mass, we petition God to send the Holy Spirit as Sanctifier to change the bread and wine into the Body and Blood of Christ and to change us, so that we, too, become holy and united in the Body of Christ.

The principal prayers of the Sacraments reveal more about the Holy Spirit's role. In Baptism, we pray to the Holy Spirit for new life. In Confirmation, we ask the Spirit to be our helper and guide. In Reconciliation, we ask the Holy Spirit, as Comforter, to forgive our sins. Through the Holy Spirit, we are given the grace to lead a Christian life.

16 The Holy Spirit Helps Us Pray

LET US PRAY

Come, Holy Spirit,
fill our hearts with your love.

Based on the Pentecost Sequence

Share

We all need teachers.
Teachers help us learn
new words.
Teachers show us how to
do new things.

Who taught you how to tie your shoelaces?

_____

_____

Who taught you how to write your name?

_____

_____

Who taught you how to ride a bike?

_____

_____

Who taught you about Jesus?

_____

_____

Who else
teaches us
how to pray?

Hear & Believe

Jesus told his friends many stories about prayer. One time, Jesus said that we should pray always.

"How can we do that?" people asked. "We will grow tired. We will run out of things to say."

Another time, Jesus explained that the Holy Spirit teaches us to pray. This Spirit helps us turn everything we say and do into a prayer. The Spirit helps us even when we feel like giving up.

"Never give up," Jesus said. "When you pray, keep asking God for what you need. Keep knocking at God's door until he answers. For everyone who asks, receives. Everyone who seeks, finds. And to everyone who knocks, the door is opened."

Based on Luke 18:1, Romans 8:26, Ephesians 6:18, and Matthew 7:7–8

Ways the Holy Spirit Helps Us

The Holy Spirit teaches us to pray. He helps us pray for what we need. We call these prayers **petitions**. Even our kind acts can become prayers. Helping a person shows our love for God. Our kind act becomes a prayer.

Activity Draw about something or someone you are praying for.

When does the Church pray to the Holy Spirit?

Hear & Believe

 Go in Peace

The Mass is almost over. We all stand up. The priest raises his hand and blesses us.

He says, "May Almighty God bless you, the Father, and the Son, and the Holy Spirit."

We make the Sign of the Cross and answer, "Amen."

Then the priest tells us to go. He says, "Go in peace to love and serve the Lord." We answer, "Thanks be to God."

The Order of Mass

The Mass is over. We go home. We ask the Holy Spirit to help us follow Jesus during the week.

? How can you love and serve others this week?

Our Church Teaches

At Mass, we pray to the Holy Spirit. We ask the Holy Spirit to help us listen to the Bible readings. The priest asks the Holy Spirit to change the bread and wine into the Body and Blood of Christ. At the end of Mass, we ask the Holy Spirit to help us share our love with others.

Activity Write the names of three people with whom you want to share your love, joy, and peace. Think about how you will do this. Close your eyes and ask the Holy Spirit to help you.

How does the Church honor the Holy Spirit?

Respond

The Holy Parade

Lucia and her grandfather are on the church steps. She hears joyful music from a band. Then she sees the marchers coming down the street.

The men and boys wear colorful shirts and vests. The women and girls wear long dresses. Each group carries a bright banner.

Lucia asks, "Why are they marching?"

"It is a holy parade, or procession," her grandfather replies. "Every year, we honor the Holy Spirit in a special way. At Mass today, we will thank God for the gift of the Holy Spirit."

? Why are the people having a procession?

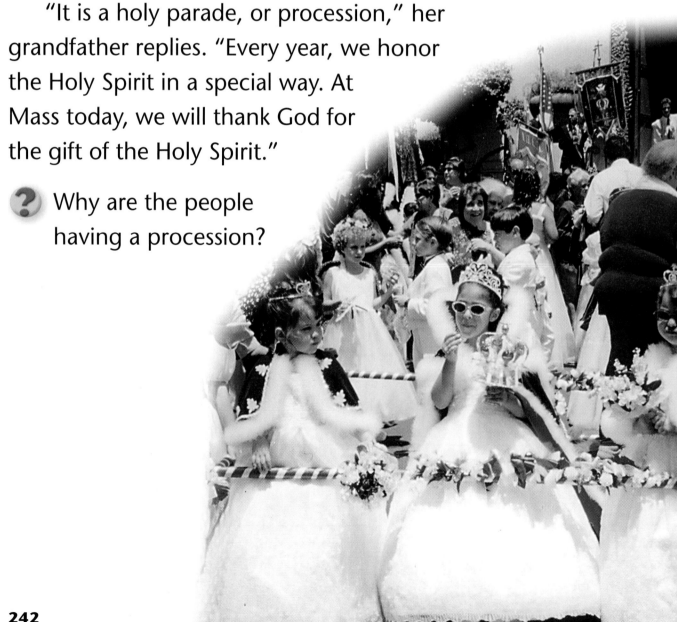

Activity

Write a petition to the Holy Spirit.
Ask the Holy Spirit to help you.
Then sign your name.

gentleness

Come, Holy Spirit,

_____

- - - - - - - - - - - - - - - - - - - -

fill me with _____ .

_____

- - - - - - - - - - - - - - - - - - - -

Help me to _____

_____

- - - - - - - - - - - - - - - - - - - -

_____ .

My name is

_____

- - - - - - - - - - - - - - - - - - - -

_____ .

peace

self-control

JOY

kindness

patience

How can we
celebrate the
Holy Spirit?

243

✝ Prayer Celebration

A Holy Spirit Procession

We can pray to the Holy Spirit with a procession. We can play music and march. Then we can pray our petitions.

Leader: Come, Holy Spirit. We know you are always with us. Please listen to our prayers.

(Children read their own petitions.)

16 Chapter Review

A **Circle** the word that best completes each sentence.

1. Helping others can be a way to _____.

   laugh   **pray**

2. Prayers that ask God for things we need are called _____.

   petitions   **praises**

3. Jesus said that we should pray _____.

   sometimes   **always**

4. The Holy Spirit teaches us to _____.

   pray   **play**

B **Write** a petition to the Holy Spirit.

Come Holy Spirit,

_____

- -

_____

_____

- -

_____

C **Complete** the sentences with words from the box.

| God | love | peace | serve |

At the end of Mass, the priest says, "Go in

_____   _____

_____ to _____ and

_____

_____ the Lord."

_____ "

We respond, "Thanks be to _____.

D **Draw or write** about one of your kind acts that can become a prayer.

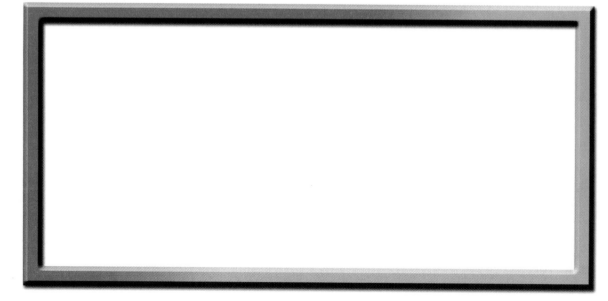

Faith in Action

Teachers   Some men and women teach in Catholic schools. They teach reading, math, and science. They also teach children about God. They read Bible stories and talk about following Jesus. The Holy Spirit guides these teachers as they share their faith.

In Your Parish

Activity   You can ask the Holy Spirit to help your teacher. Learn this prayer. Color the border. Then pray for your teacher.

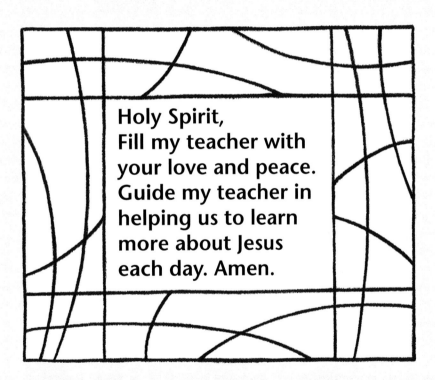

Holy Spirit,
Fill my teacher with your love and peace. Guide my teacher in helping us to learn more about Jesus each day. Amen.

In Everyday Life

Activity   The Holy Spirit helps us share our faith with others. What could you tell someone in your family about Jesus? What could you tell a friend about the Mass?

Faith in Action

Altar Servers   Boys and girls can usually become altar servers in the fourth grade. If they are in the parish school, they can serve at both parish and school Masses. An altar server carries the crucifix in the processions. The servers help set the altar for Mass.

In Your Parish

Activity   In each corner of the maze, there is something to bring to the altar. Draw a line along the right path from each object to the altar.

In Everyday Life

Activity   Name two ways that you can serve, or help, your family at home. Name two ways you can serve at school.

Faith in Action

Youth Group Many parishes have a group for teens. The teens make new friends, serve their community, and learn more about God. Some teens visit the sick. Some collect clothes for the poor. Others rake leaves or shovel snow for older members of the parish.

In Your Parish

Activity Does your parish have a youth group? How do the teens help people?

In Everyday Life

Activity
The Holy Spirit helps us act in good ways. Read the signs. Circle one way that you would like to act. Then draw yourself acting in this way.

Help a friend.

Share your toys.

Pray every day.

Obey your parents.

Forgive others.

Faith in Action

Prayer Box Many parishes have a "Prayer Box." People write petitions on small cards and put them in the box. When a prayer group meets, the members read some of the petitions. Then the group prays for the needs of the people.

In Your Parish

Activity How does your parish pray for the needs of its people? Is there a prayer box? Find out. Then you can pray for people's needs, too.

In Everyday Life

Activity Look at the Prayer Chain. On each link, write the name of a person who needs prayers. Then pray for these people.

Prayer Chain

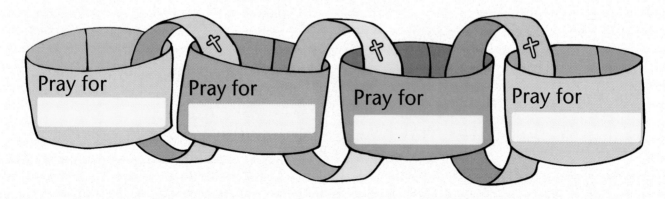

Pray for

Pray for

Pray for

Pray for

We celebrate the gift of the Holy Spirit.

The Holy Spirit is our helper.

Jesus promises the Holy Spirit.

The Holy Spirit helps us pray.

Read the sentences on the posters.

1 Find the poster that tells who the Holy Spirit is.
Color the border yellow.

2 Find the poster that tells who Jesus promises us.
Color the border red.

3 Find the poster that tells how the Holy Spirit helps us.
Color the border green.

4 Find the poster that tells what we celebrate.
Color the border blue.

A **Write** the number of each question in the box before the answer.

1. Whom did God send to be with us always as our helper and guide?

☐ **Christians**

2. What are the special signs of God's love?

☐ **petitions**

3. Which Sacrament makes our faith in Jesus Christ stronger?

☐ **Sacraments**

4. Which people love Jesus Christ and follow him?

☐ **Holy Spirit**

5. What prayers ask God for things we need?

☐ **Confirmation**

B **Circle** the name that completes each sentence.

1. The young saint who helped boys at his school make peace with one another was ____.

   Francis   **Dominic Savio**

2. The man who asked Jesus how to become a member of God's family was ____.

   Nicodemus   **Augustine**

3. The saint who taught people how to use the Fruits of the Holy Spirit was ____.

   Katharine Drexel   **Thomas Aquinas**

4. The saint who wrote letters to the first Christians about the Holy Spirit was ____.

   Philip   **Paul**

C **Write** one way you can use a Fruit of the Holy Spirit to help someone.

D **Complete** the sentences with words from the box.

water	Fruits	Holy Spirit
pray	God's life	

1. The _____ is a gift
of God's love.

2. In Baptism, _____ is a sign
of new life.

3. Jesus said that _____
lasts forever.

4. The _____ of the Holy Spirit help
us show love to others.

5. The Holy Spirit teaches us to _____.

Jesus' Church of Followers

The Catholic Church throughout the world helps people in need. These people are our brothers and sisters. As baptized Christians, we are called to love and serve others.

Go into the whole world. Share the Good News about Jesus with everyone.

Based on Mark 16:15

Early Christians traveled this road to faraway countries. They helped people learn about Jesus. These children are helping by sending clothes to needy people around the world.

Laudate Dominum

Psalm 117, "Praise the Lord, all you peoples."

Music by *Jacques Berthier*

OSTINATO REFRAIN

Lau - da - te Do - mi-num, lau - da - te Do - mi-num

om - nes gen-tes, al - le - lu – ia. al - le - lu – ia.

© 1980, Les Presses de Taizé, GIA Publications, Inc., agent.

Take Home

Jesus' Followers Become the Church

In this chapter, the children will learn that Jesus invites his followers to belong to the Church. From the Scripture story, the children will discover that the first Christians prayed together, celebrated the Eucharist, and helped poor people. The children will also learn that the word *Amen* means "Yes, I believe. It is true."

ACTIVITY

Family Traditions Tell your children stories about relatives who were role models for the way your family prays, celebrates, and helps others. If you have letters or photos about these traditions, share them with your children.

WEEKLY PLANNER

On Sunday
Discuss how your church building is like a home for your parish community.

On the Web
blestarewe.com
Visit our Web site for the saint of the day and the reflection question of the week.

Saint of the Week

 Saint Peter the Apostle (first century)

Peter, a fisherman, was called by Jesus to be one of his Twelve Apostles. Jesus loved Peter very much, even though Peter denied knowing him on the night Jesus was arrested. After his Resurrection, Jesus appointed Peter leader of the Apostles and head of the Church. Peter was later arrested in Rome and put to death.

Feast Day: February 22

 A Prayer for the Week

Lord Jesus Christ, we thank you for calling us to be your followers. Send us your Spirit to fill us with joy and to help us share our love with others. Amen.

Take Home

FAMILY TIME

✝ Scripture Background

In the Time of the Early Church

The Eucharist   Scripture provides few details about how the Eucharist, or Lord's Supper, was celebrated in the early Church. From brief accounts, we sense that the disciples were filled with the joy of the Resurrection and the hope of the Second Coming. Each day they gathered in someone's home for a communal meal at which they thanked God and recalled the events of Jesus' life, Death, and Resurrection. By repeating Jesus' words at the Last Supper, he became present to them in the breaking of bread.

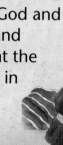

Read about the first celebrations of the Eucharist in Acts 2:42–47 and 1 Corinthians 11:17–34.

OUR CATHOLIC TRADITION in Architecture

Domed Churches   In Eastern Christianity, churches are usually topped with domes instead of steeples. These domes are often gilded, expressing the radiance of Heaven. One of the most famous of the domed churches is the Cathedral of St. Basil in Moscow, Russia. The building of the cathedral began in the sixteenth century during the reign of Czar Ivan IV. Its many colorful, onion-shaped domes are covered with intricate patterns, and gold is used heavily in the decoration.

17 Jesus' Followers Become the Church

Jesus' followers were filled with joy and the Holy Spirit.

Based on Acts 13:52

Share

Our friends bring joy to our lives.

We can do things with our friends.

We can share things with our friends.

We can tell our friends how we feel.

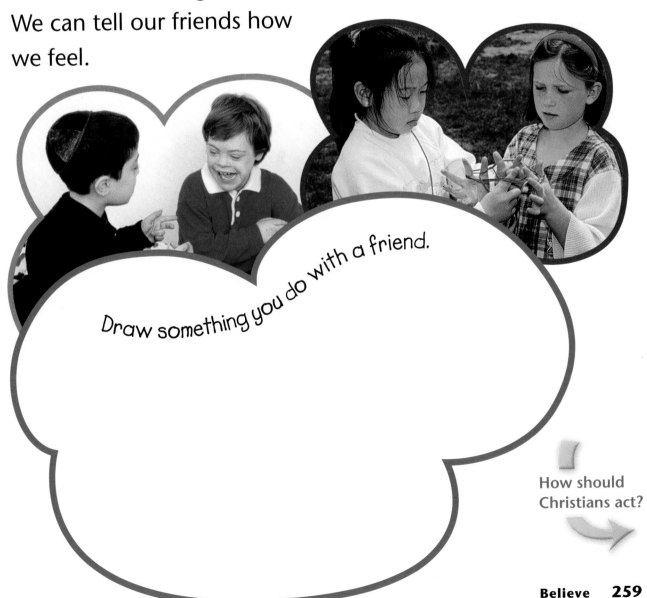

Draw something you do with a friend.

How should Christians act?

Hear & Believe

✝ Scripture The First Christians

After Christ rose from the dead, many people began to believe in him. They became his followers. Here is what these first Christians did.

They listened to the Apostles. They tried to live and act like Jesus. They prayed together and celebrated the Eucharist. They shared their food with each other. They helped people who were poor. They grew in faith and brought joy to one another.

Based on Acts 2:42–47

Acting as Christians

The followers of Jesus became the first members of the Church. They loved one another. Their **faith**, or belief in God, was strong. Jesus calls us, too, to be members of his Church. When we show love to others, we are true Christians.

Activity Complete the sentence.

Write one way you can show love to others.

I show love to others when I

_____

- -

_____
_____

- -

_____.

How do members of the Church care for one another?

Hear & Believe

Christians Care

Early one morning, Sister Helen's phone rang. She picked up the phone and listened. Someone told her a very sad story.

Mr. Ames was in a car accident. He died on the way to the hospital. Mr. Ames was the father of two children in Holy Family School.

Sister Helen knew that the Ames family would need help. She called Mrs. Lewis, a member of the parish. Mrs. Lewis leads a group that helps out when a family member dies. She knew just what to do.

Mrs. Lewis called the members of her group. Soon the Ames family had the help they needed. They felt that people really cared.

? How do you think the people of Holy Family Parish helped the Ames family?

Our Church Teaches

As Catholics, our faith helps us believe what our Church teaches. We say "**Amen**" to show that we believe. *Amen* is a prayer often prayed by the first Christians. We pray "Amen" many times at Mass. We pray "Amen" at the end of prayers we say each day. *Amen* means "Yes, I believe. It is true."

Activity Color the letters to show how you feel when you pray "Amen."

Faith Words

Amen

Amen means "Yes, I believe. It is true." We often say "Amen" at the end of prayers.

How can we act like the first Christians?

Respond

Saint Paul's Parish

The people of Saint Paul's parish try to act like the first Christians. Here are some ways they show love to others.

Mrs. Santos teaches children about Jesus.

Nancy prays with others.

Vanessa takes care of young children.

Activity

There are six words in the Word Search.

The words tell what Christians should do.

Find the words and circle them.

L	I	S	T	E	N
E	Z	H	B	Q	W
A	T	A	L	K	P
R	P	R	A	Y	U
N	H	E	L	P	V

Mrs. Carr helps people who are poor.

Ryan listens to a friend

Mr. Smith drives senior citizens to lunch.

How can we pray "Amen"?

Prayer Celebration

A Prayer of Faith

Amen is a Christian prayer of faith. When we pray "Amen," we say "yes" to God. We say that we believe.

Let us pray "Amen" to what we believe.

Reader 1: Thank you, God, for the gift of the Church. We believe you want us to belong to the Catholic Church.

All: Amen.

Reader 2: Thank you, God, for the gift of creation. We believe you know us and care for us.

All: Amen.

Reader 3: Thank you, God, for the gift of Jesus. We believe he is your Son.

All: Amen.

Reader 4: Thank you, God, for the gift of the Holy Spirit. We believe your Spirit is always with us.

All: Amen.

A **Draw a line** to connect the parts of each sentence.

1. The first Christians tried to live and act ● ● of the Church.

2. Belief and trust in God is called ● ● like Jesus.

3. We end prayers with the word ● ● faith.

4. Jesus' followers became members ● ● Amen.

B **Write or draw** about one way people in your parish act as Christians.

C **Draw a line** to connect each word with the picture that shows the way a Christian acts.

1. listen •

2. pray •

3. share •

4. help •

D **Write** the word that means "I believe" and "It is true."

_____

- -

_____

Take Home

FAMILY TIME

We Celebrate Pentecost

In this chapter, the children will recognize the Feast of Pentecost as the birthday of the Church. They will hear the Scripture story of how the Holy Spirit filled Jesus' followers with the gift of God's love. The children will discover that people from all over the world belong to the Catholic Church, and will discuss what it means to live in peace.

ACTIVITY

A Pentecost Mobile With your child, make a Pentecost mobile out of a hanger, thread, and red and white construction paper. Cut out a white dove and red flames. Label each flame with a family member's name. Using thread, hang the dove and flames from the hanger. The dove symbolizes God's power to make us holy, and the flames represent the outpouring of the Holy Spirit.

WEEKLY PLANNER

On Sunday

Find out how your parish plans to celebrate Pentecost by asking a member of the parish staff or looking in the parish bulletin.

On the Web

blestarewe.com

Visit our Web site for the saint of the day and the reflection question of the week.

Saint of the Week

Saint Francis Xavier (1506–1552)

Francis Xavier grew up in Spain and studied in Paris. He helped his friend, Ignatius, found the Society of Jesus, or Jesuits. Francis worked with the poor and sick in India and Japan. He learned their languages and baptized over one thousand people.

Patron Saint of: missionaries in foreign lands

Feast Day: December 3

A Prayer for the Week

God our Father, we thank you for sending us your Holy Spirit. Help our family follow the example of Saint Francis Xavier by telling others about the Good News of Jesus. Amen.

Take Home

FAMILY TIME

✝ Scripture Background

In the Time of the Early Church

Pentecost   In the Old Testament, Pentecost was celebrated as the Feast of Weeks. It began as an agricultural feast, showing gratitude to God for the early harvest. The feast was held fifty days after the first day of Passover. In the New Testament, Christians began to celebrate Pentecost as a commemoration of the day the Church was born. On this day, the Holy Spirit came to the Apostles and empowered them to speak in tongues. People from many countries were able to understand the Good News about Jesus in their own languages.

You can read the account of the first Pentecost in Acts 2:1–42.

OUR CATHOLIC TRADITION in Culture

Pentecost Around the World

The celebration of Pentecost differs around the world. In Italy, it was customary to throw rose leaves from church ceilings to symbolize the fiery tongues. In France, trumpets were blown to recall the sound of the mighty wind that came with the descent of the Holy Spirit.

Today in Eastern Catholic Churches, the Vespers of Pentecost includes a ritual of genuflection. In Russia, people carry flowers and green branches in a procession. The photo shows pilgrims journeying to the annual Pentecost festival held in El Rocio in southern Spain.

18 We Celebrate Pentecost

LET US PRAY The Holy Spirit fills the whole world.

Based on Wisdom 1:7

Share

Birthdays are very special days.
Our families and friends celebrate with us.
They are glad that we belong to them.
When is your birthday?

_____

- -

_____

Month   **Day**

Circle the things that were part of your last birthday celebration.

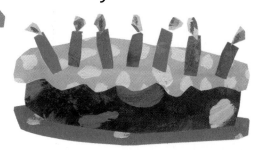

Draw another special thing that was at your birthday celebration.

When does the Church celebrate its birthday?

Hear & Believe

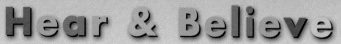

🕯 Worship The Church's Birthday

A reading from the Acts of the Apostles

Fifty days after Easter, Jesus' followers were praying together. Suddenly there was a sound like a great wind blowing. The noise filled the whole house. Then flames, like tongues of fire, appeared over each person's head. The Holy Spirit filled all the people in the house with God's love. The Apostles and the others rushed outside. They began telling everyone about Jesus.

Outside there were people from many countries. These people spoke different languages. But they all understood what Jesus' followers were saying.

Based on Acts 2:1–6

Reader: The word of the Lord.

All: Thanks be to God.

Our Church Teaches

The Church welcomes people of all races, languages, and abilities. Today people all over the world belong to the Church. As Catholics, we try to live in **peace** with everyone.

Activity At Mass, we give one another a Sign of Peace. Write the words you say.

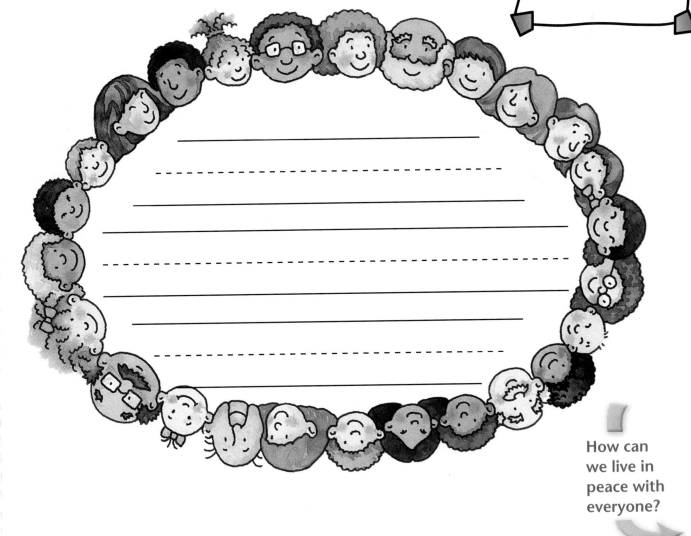

How can we live in peace with everyone?

Respond

The Special Sunday

Pentecost is a special Sunday in Sylvia's parish. The children are invited to walk in a procession. They carry flags from many countries. Sylvia carries a flag from Mexico. Her friend Ravi carries the flag of India. The flags remind everyone that the Church is made up of people from all over the world.

During Mass, the people sing in different languages. After Mass, everyone goes outside to eat foods and play games from different countries.

? What did the people in Sylvia's parish celebrate on Pentecost?

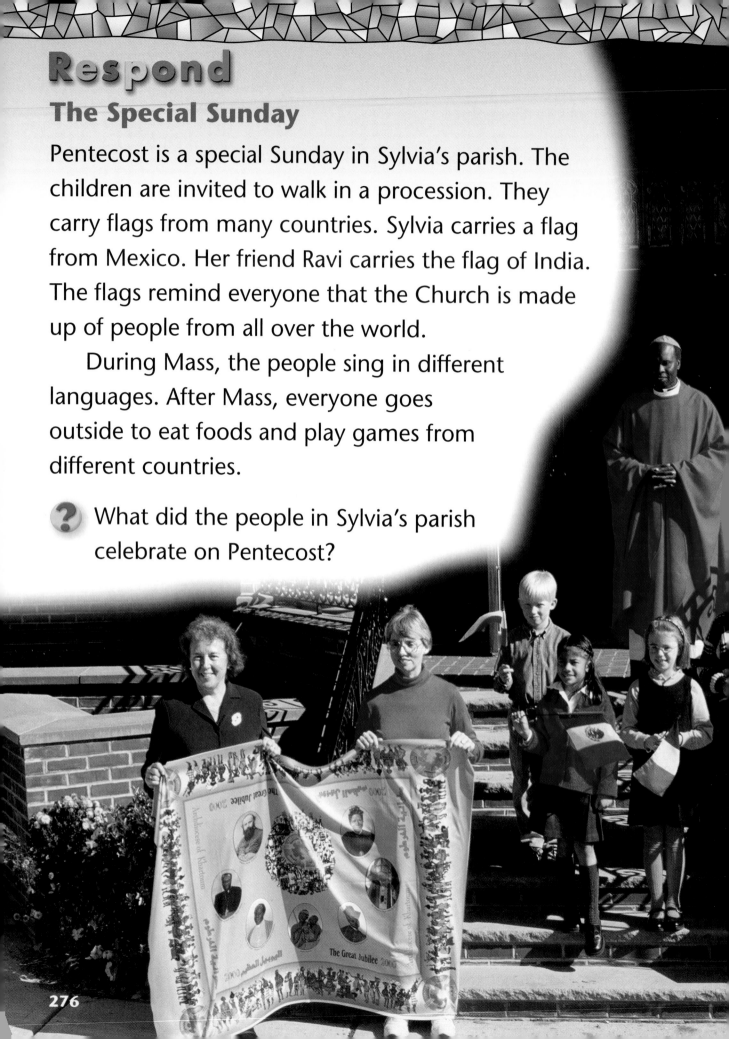

Activity

1. Many different people make up the Church. Many colors make a beautiful picture. Use this code to color the picture. What do you see?

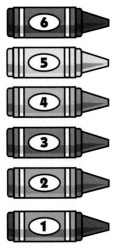

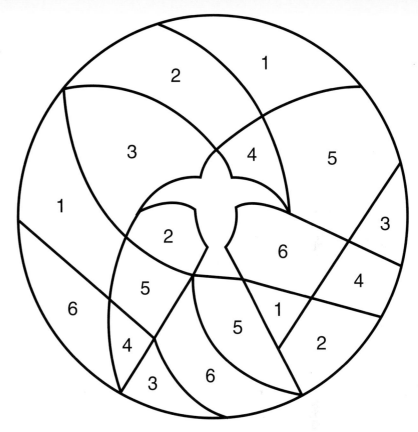

2. Circle the words that tell ways to keep peace.

You are playing a game with a friend.

cheat   **play fair**

A friend calls you names.

forgive   **act mad**

There is one toy, but three people.

take it   **share it**

A family member needs you.

help   **watch TV**

How can we celebrate the Church's birthday?

✝ Prayer Celebration

A Silent Prayer

We believe the Holy Spirit lives in us. Silence helps us feel God's nearness and love. One way to become silent is by relaxing our bodies. We can relax by closing our eyes and breathing very slowly.

Breathe in: 1, 2, 3, 4, 5, 6

Hold your breath: 1, 2, 3

Breathe out: 1, 2, 3, 4, 5, 6

(*Repeat 3 or 4 times.*)

Now, be still and listen to God in your heart.

Feel the love and peace of the Holy Spirit.

A **Complete** the sentences with words from the box.

| Holy Spirit   Jesus   Pentecost   peace   Apostles |

1. The birthday of the Church is called

   _____

   -

   _____.

2. Pentecost celebrates the coming of the

   _____

   -

   _____.

3. The Holy Spirit filled the followers of

   _____

   -

   _____ with God's love.

4. The Holy Spirit helped the

   _____

   -

   _____ teach people

   of all countries about Jesus.

5. Silent prayer can help us feel the love and

   _____

   -

   _____ of the Holy Spirit.

B **Write or draw** about how we can celebrate the Church's birthday.

C **Write or draw** about how Saint Francis Xavier was a follower of Jesus.

Take Home

FAMILY TIME

The Church Helps the World

Our Church teaches that all the people in the world are our brothers and sisters. In this chapter, the children will learn that our mission as Christians is to love and serve others. They will discover how Catholics have answered God's call to help people all over the world. The children will become aware of ways they can help people in need, and of the importance of praying for our Church's "helpers."

ACTIVITY

Cards Full of Cheer Help your child make cheerful cards for children in a hospital or elderly people in a nursing home. Deliver the cards yourselves, or give the cards to someone in your parish who will deliver them.

WEEKLY PLANNER

On Sunday

Check your parish's bulletin or Web site to find out how your parish is reaching out to help poor people around the world.

On the Web

blestarewe.com

 Visit our Web site for the saint of the day and the reflection question of the week.

Saint of the Week

 Blessed Teresa of Calcutta (1910–1997)

Mother Teresa, was born Gonxha Agnes Bojaxhiu in Yugoslavia. At eighteen, she entered the Sisters of Loreto and became a high school teacher in Calcutta, India. In 1948 she felt God calling her to serve the poorest of the poor, and founded the Missionaries of Charity. Today members of this community serve the poor, sick, and dying around the world.

Feast Day: September 5

A Prayer for the Week

Lord, we want to help people in need. Help us to be your hands and feet in the world today. Give us courage to answer your call to serve others. Amen.

Take Home

FAMILY TIME

✝ Scripture Background

In the Time of the Early Church

The Role of Deacons As the early Church grew in numbers, the Apostles found they were no longer able to see to all the needs of the faithful. Therefore, they asked the disciples to choose several reputable men from the community to assist them. The Apostles ordained those chosen as deacons. The deacons performed services connected to the ritual of the Lord's Supper, such as serving and cleaning up. They also cared for the needs of widows and orphans.

You can read more about deacons in 1 Timothy 3:8–13.

OUR CATHOLIC TRADITION in Holy People

A Witness to the Poor

Dorothy Day was a convert to Catholicism who had a strong sense of the social call of the Gospel. She reached out to the poor and powerless, and gave of herself with great dignity. She started Catholic Worker houses across the country, and encouraged people to follow Christ.

Among the groups of people Dorothy ministered to were women prisoners. While she was visiting a West Virginia prison, an elderly inmate wanted to know why Dorothy was there. She replied that she had come to wash their feet. Dorothy Day died in 1980. She was a powerful witness to the Church's mission of serving the poor.

19 The Church Helps the World

Go into the whole world. Share the Good News about Jesus with everyone.

Based on Mark 16:15

Share

Before we can help others, we must find out what they need. Look at these pictures. What do the people need?

He needs

_____

- -

_____.

They need

_____

- -

_____.

She needs

_____

- - - - - - - - - - - - - - - - - -

_____.

Why should Christians help people in need?

Live 283

Hear & Believe

✝ Scripture The Need for Helpers

The Church of Jesus' followers grew quickly. There was too much work for the Apostles to do by themselves. So they asked the community to choose helpers. Some of these helpers were Stephen, Philip, and Nicholas. Stephen was good at telling people about God's Word in the Bible. The others made sure the people had food, clothes, and a place to live.

Then the Apostles had time to tell more people about Jesus. They had more time to lead people in prayer and to spread the Word of God.

Based on Acts 6:1–7

Christian Service

The first Christians learned that God calls everyone to help and **serve** others. They took care of everyone in their community. Helping people is our **mission**, too. When we take care of the needs of others, we follow Jesus.

Activity These words tell about our mission to help others. Learn to sign the words.

Christians   love and serve   others.

How can we serve others?

Hear & Believe

Called to Serve

Laura went to college to learn how to be a teacher. She loved children and wanted to help them. Laura heard about the Jesuit Volunteers at school. Jesuit Volunteers serve poor people all over the world. Some volunteers are teachers or nurses. Others are young adults like the young woman in the picture. They love God and want to serve the poor.

Laura said yes to God's call. She became a Jesuit Volunteer. Laura was sent to teach children at a Catholic school in Peru. She worked there for two years. She helped many children. Laura helped their families, too.

? Why did Laura become a Jesuit Volunteer?

Our Church Teaches

All the people in the world are our brothers and sisters. Many people need help. Each baptized person is called to love and serve others. The Holy Spirit helps us serve others with love, peace, and joy.

Activity Write or draw about how you could help others when you grow up.

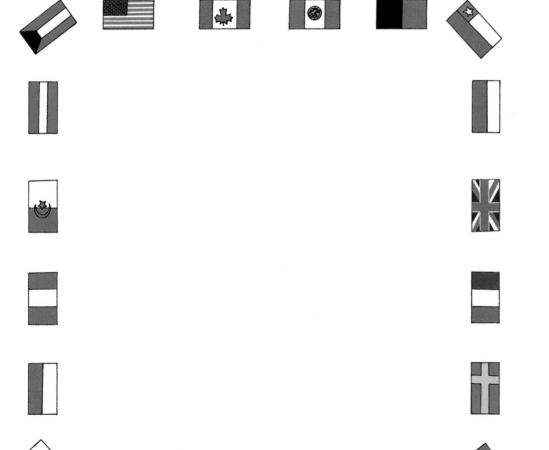

How does the Church help people in need?

Respond

Catholics Help Others

The Catholic Church helps people all over the world. Some Catholics serve in countries far away. They help people by giving them food, clothes, and medicine. They teach people how to read and write. They tell people about Jesus.

Some Catholics serve in their own country. They build houses for the poor. They serve food to homeless people. They also teach people about Jesus.

? How can we help our Church's helpers?

Activity

1. Draw how you can help someone in need.

2. Write a prayer for church helpers who serve the needs of others.

How can we get ready to be God's helpers?

Prayer Celebration

Saying "Yes" to God

Leader: As you grow up, God asks you to love and serve others. Are you listening? Are you ready to say "yes" to God?

Let us pray about saying "yes" to God.

All: God, our Creator, you called us by name to belong to your Church. As we grow up, help us to hear your voice. Give us the courage to say "yes" to your call. Amen.

A **Circle** the words that best complete the sentences.

1. God calls everyone to _____ others.

   serve   **hurt**

2. We believe that _____ in the world are our brothers and sisters.

   some people   **all people**

3. As baptized persons, our _____ is to help others.

   mission   **nation**

4. The Holy Spirit helps us serve others with _____.

   gifts and money   **love and joy**

B **Draw or write** about how a Catholic today can answer God's call to serve others.

C **Draw a line** to match each sentence about a person who needs help to the correct church helper.

1. A boy needs something to keep him warm. •

•

2. A sick woman needs medicine. •

•

3. Children in Africa want to learn how to read. •

•

4. A man needs food for his family. •

•

Take Home

FAMILY TIME

We Pray with Holy Songs

By incorporating music into our prayer, we add a new dimension to the way we relate to God. This chapter encourages the children to think of church music as an integral part of our worship experience. They will discover that holy songs are prayers, and that when we sing with our hearts, as well as our voices, we pray twice.

ACTIVITY

Feel the Music Play a song that your child likes. Have fun listening to the music and singing the words. Dance to the music with your child, expressing how the song makes you feel.

WEEKLY PLANNER

On Sunday

During Mass, listen carefully to the words of the hymns. After Mass, discuss how they relate to the Scripture readings.

On the Web

blestarewe.com

Visit our Web site for the saint of the day and the reflection question of the week.

Saint of the Week

Saint Cecilia
(? third century)

According to legend, Cecilia lived in Rome at a time of great persecution. At her wedding, she sang hymns in her heart. Cecilia was responsible for the conversion of her pagan husband and his brother. All three were martyred. Cecilia is often pictured playing a harp or an organ. Many church choirs bear her name.

Patron Saint of: musicians
Feast Day: November 22

A Prayer for the Week

Dear God, we thank you for the gift of music. It comforts us when we feel sad and helps us express our joy. Help us lift our hearts and minds to you in song. Amen.

Take Home

FAMILY TIME

✚ Scripture Background

Before the Time of Jesus and in the Early Church

Musical Instruments The most frequently mentioned biblical instrument is the shofar, or ram's horn, which is still used in synagogues today. The kinnor, or David's harp, in the Old Testament was actually a lyre, used to accompany the praying of the Psalms. Instruments mentioned in the New Testament include the harp, the flute, the lyre, the trumpet, and cymbals. The "resounding gong" referred to by Paul in 1 Corinthians 13:1, were actually vases set up to amplify actors' voices in Greek theaters.

You can read about the importance of religious music to the first Christians in Ephesians 5:18–20.

OUR CATHOLIC TRADITION in Music

Spirituals Most African slaves in our country were not allowed to learn how to read or write. Many slaves were converted to Christianity. One way they kept their faith alive was by singing spirituals. These songs, based on Scripture, sustained the slaves in the same way the Psalms sustained the Israelites during their captivity. The spirituals also helped slaves pass on their faith. Spirituals are now considered an art form, and one of the original forms of music on this continent. As African Americans became Catholics, they brought with them their rich heritage in these biblically based hymns.

20 We Pray with Holy Songs

My heart is full of joy.
I sing praises to my God.

Based on Psalm 28:7

Share

People sing for many reasons.

Songs put babies to sleep.

Songs remind us of our country.

Songs take away our fears.

Songs celebrate happy times.

What is your favorite song?

_____

- -

_____

Why do
Christians
sing?

Hear & Believe

✝ Scripture Songs of the First Christians

When the first Christians celebrated the Eucharist, they did several things. They read the Bible. They prayed. They received the Body and Blood of Jesus. And they sang songs.

Why did they sing? Here is what Paul told the first Christians.

Be filled with God's Spirit. Sing psalms and hymns to God the Father. Sing your thanks and praise to God in the name of our Lord Jesus Christ.

Based on Ephesians 5:18–19

Our Church Teaches

We sing hymns at Mass to praise and thank God. Many of the words we sing come from the Psalms and stories in the Bible. These holy songs help lift our hearts to God.

Activity We sing Amen to show that we believe what our Church teaches. Learn to sing the notes below. Then color the border.

Amen

Marty Haugen

A - men, a - men,

a - men!

© 1984, G.I.A. Publications, Inc. All rights reserved. Used with permission.

How can we sing our thanks and praise to God?

Respond

Amanda Loves to Sing

Amanda loves to sing at church. She sings as her parish community gathers to praise God. After the first Bible reading, she sings a psalm. She sings a hymn when people bring the bread and wine to the altar. She prays to God our Father, when she sings the Lord's Prayer. Amanda sings at Communion time. She also sings at the end of Mass.

Sometimes during the week, Amanda hums or sings the songs from Mass. The music reminds her to give God thanks and praise. It reminds her to live in peace. It helps her love and serve others.

? What holy songs do you like to hum or sing?

Activity

Use these words to complete the sentences.
Then write the words in the puzzle.

| hymn | praise | pray | psalm | thanks |

DOWN

1. We give God

th_____ _____.

3. Singing is a

____ ____ ____ ____

way to ____ ____ ____ ____.

ACROSS

2. By singing, we

____ ____ ____ ____ ____ ____

____ ____ ____ ____ ____ ____ God.

____ ____ ____ ____ ____

3. A ____ ____ ____ ____ ____ is
a song that is also a prayer.

____ ____ ____ ____

4. A ____ ____ ____ ____ is a holy song.

How can we
celebrate our
good year?

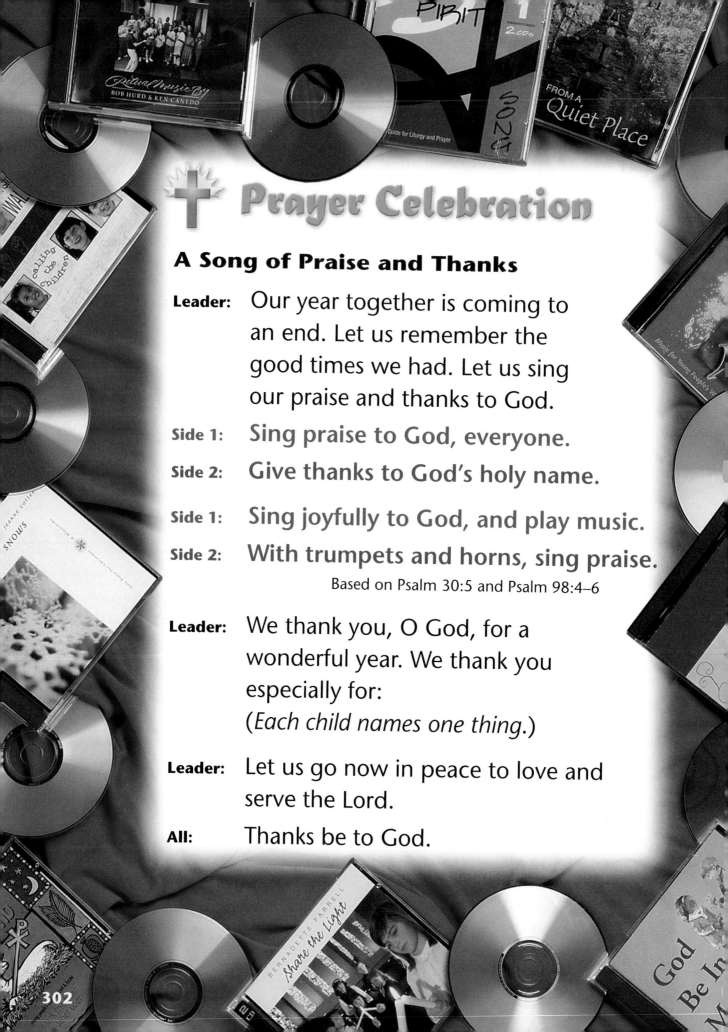

✝ Prayer Celebration

A Song of Praise and Thanks

Leader: Our year together is coming to an end. Let us remember the good times we had. Let us sing our praise and thanks to God.

Side 1: Sing praise to God, everyone.

Side 2: Give thanks to God's holy name.

Side 1: Sing joyfully to God, and play music.

Side 2: With trumpets and horns, sing praise.

Based on Psalm 30:5 and Psalm 98:4–6

Leader: We thank you, O God, for a wonderful year. We thank you especially for:
(*Each child names one thing.*)

Leader: Let us go now in peace to love and serve the Lord.

All: Thanks be to God.

A **Draw a line** to the word that best completes each sentence.

1. Holy songs are called ●   ● praise.

2. When we sing holy songs, we pray ●   ● hymns.

3. Catholics sing holy songs at ●   ● twice.

4. Holy songs give God thanks and ●   ● Mass.

B **Circle** the word that best completes each sentence.

1. Paul told the first Christians to sing ____ to God.

   stories   **psalms**

2. The first Christians sang because the Holy Spirit filled them with ____.

   sorrow   **joy**

3. Holy songs can lift our ____ to God.

   hearts   **hands**

4. Holy songs can remind us to live in ____.

   fear   **peace**

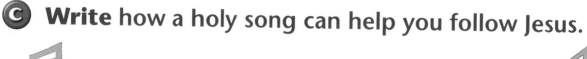
C **Write** how a holy song can help you follow Jesus.

_____

- -

_____

- -

_____

D **Write or draw** one way Saint Cecilia
shared the joy of the Holy Spirit with others.

Faith in Action

Job-Finding Helpers If someone needs a job, Mount Carmel Parish tries to help. The parish Web site lists many job openings. A person can sign up on the Web site. The job-finding group can help a person learn new skills. That can help the person get a job.

In Your Parish

Activity Mr. Mann lost his job as a carpenter. His wife is ill and cannot work. Their children need clothes. How could your parish help?

In Everyday Life

Activity The words in the box name our rights. Find and circle each right in the Word Search.

food

shoes

home

school

doctor

job

c	o	f	o	o	d	i	u
z	s	o	b	r	o	g	y
y	c	i	f	q	c	s	p
k	h	o	m	e	t	j	z
k	o	e	h	j	o	b	d
y	o	o	j	n	r	l	o
j	l	z	o	e	c	s	u
l	o	s	h	o	e	s	z

Faith in Action

Readers of God's Word At Mass, we listen to readings from the Bible. The people who read the Word of God are called lectors. At home, they learn about the Bible stories. They practice reading the stories aloud. The lectors want us to hear God's message. They want us to believe the words we hear.

In Your Parish

Activity On Pentecost, a lector reads aloud the Bible story about the coming of the Holy Spirit.
Circle the words in the box that are in the Pentecost story. Then tell the story in your own words.

fifty days   Christmas   Easter   followers   water

eating   praying   flames   wind   God's love

Apostles   Holy Spirit   children   animals

languages   Jesus   people

Temple   Church

born

In Everyday Life

Activity Choose a favorite Bible story from your book. Read the story to yourself. Then pretend you are a lector. Read the Word of God to others.

Faith in Action

Rosary for Peace Each week, the fifth graders in Saint Lucy's School visit a nearby nursing home. They pray the Rosary with a group of Catholic people in the home. When they say "Holy Mary, Mother of God, pray for us," a child holds up a picture of a place in the world that needs peace. They ask for Mary's help.

In Your Parish

Activity At Sunday Mass, your parish prays for peace in the world. Think of a place that needs peace. Make up your own prayer for peace.

In Everyday Life

Activity Write or draw about a way you can be a peacemaker in your family, school, or neighborhood.

Faith in Action

Music Director The music director in Saint John's Parish also works with the school children. She chooses hymns that go with the Bible readings at the school Mass each Friday. She helps the children learn new songs. The music director tells them to sing from their hearts. She invites them to sing their praise to God.

In Your Parish

Activity Write a thank you note to the music director in your parish. Tell how you feel about the holy songs that are sung at Mass.

In Everyday Life

Activity Think about your favorite hymn, or holy song. Very quietly, sing the words to yourself. Tell how this song can help you pray.

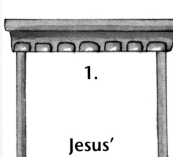
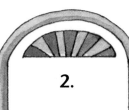

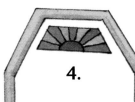

1. Jesus' Followers Become the Church

2. We Celebrate Pentecost

3. The Church Helps the World

4. We Pray with Holy Songs

Read the titles on the doors.

The sentences below tell about things
you learned in one of the chapters.

Write the correct door number on each knob.

 This day is the Church's birthday.
The Holy Spirit came on this day.

 The first Christians grew in faith.
They prayed "Amen."

 We pray with our voices and our hearts.
We sing praise and thanks to God.

 The Church has many missions.
The Catholic Church needs helpers.

Unit Review

A **Find** the letter hidden in each picture. **Fill in** the missing letter to make the word that means "Yes, I believe. It is true."
Then **color** the letters and the pictures.

  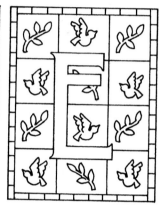 

B **Find** the letter hidden in each picture. **Fill in** the missing letters to make the word that means "belief and trust in God."
Then **color** the letters and the pictures.

  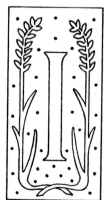  

c **Complete** each sentence with a word from the box.

peace	mission	silent	Pentecost	hymns

1. We celebrate the coming of the Holy Spirit

_____

on _____ .

2. As Christians, our _____

is to love and serve others.

3. All Catholics should try to live in

_____

_____ with everyone.

4. A _____ prayer

can help us feel the love and peace of the
Holy Spirit.

5. Holy songs that lift our hearts to God

_____

are called _____ .

D **Draw a line** to the correct answer to each question.

1. Who helped the
   Apostles teach people
   about Jesus?   ●   ● Saint Cecilia

2. Who told the first
   Christians to sing
   psalms and hymns
   to God?   ●   ● the Holy Spirit

3. Who showed Christians   ●   ● Saint Francis
   in Rome how to pray   Xavier
   with music?

4. Who baptized many   ●   ● Saint Paul
   people in India
   and Japan?

E **Write** one way you can answer God's call
   to serve others.

   _____

   -

   _____

   -

   _____

FEASTS AND SEASONS

the Church Year

The calendar of the Catholic Church is made up of special seasons. The weeks of each season celebrate the life and teachings of Jesus Christ.

Holy Week begins on Palm Sunday. It ends with three holy days that remind us of the Last Supper, and that Jesus died and rose to new life to save all people.

HOLY WEEK

Our church year begins on the first Sunday of **Advent**. We have four weeks to get ready to celebrate Jesus' birthday on Christmas.

ADVENT

ADVENT

The church year begins.

ORDINARY TIME

In the second part of **Ordinary Time**, we learn more about the life and teachings of Jesus.

The **Easter** season is a time of great joy. It begins on Easter Sunday. Easter Time lasts for fifty days. We celebrate that Jesus was raised from the dead. We sing, "Alleluia!"

EASTER

The season of **Lent** lasts forty days. During Lent, we get ready for Easter. We pray, give up things, and share what we have with others.

In the first part of **Ordinary Time**, we learn how Jesus began his work among the people.

LENT   **ORDINARY TIME**

During the **Christmas** season, we celebrate that Jesus, the Son of God, came to earth as our Savior.

CHRISTMAS

Why Sunday Is a Special Day

Our Church celebrates Sunday as the most special day of the week. At Mass, we remember that Jesus died to save us. We remember that he was raised from the dead on Easter Sunday. That is why Sunday is called "the Lord's Day."

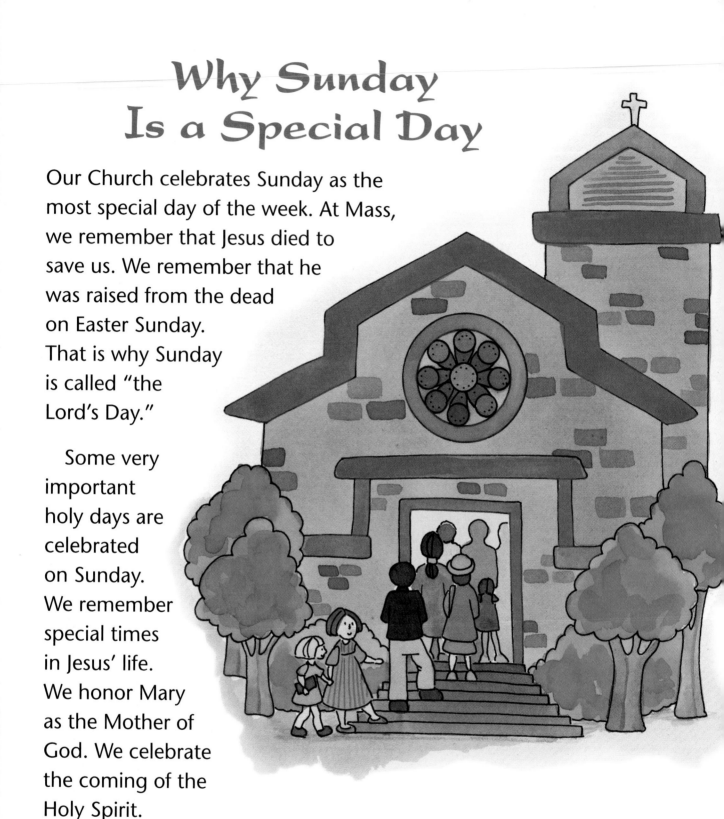

Some very important holy days are celebrated on Sunday. We remember special times in Jesus' life. We honor Mary as the Mother of God. We celebrate the coming of the Holy Spirit.

Because Sunday is the Lord's Day, we take time to relax. We spend time with our family and friends. We try to be helpful and kind.

Colors of the Church Year

Each time a priest celebrates Mass, he puts on clothes called vestments. One of the vestments is called a chasuble. It looks like a beautiful poncho. The color of the chasuble changes with each season of the church year.

Purple or violet is for Advent and Lent. White or gold is for Christmas and Easter. Red is for special days like Palm Sunday, Good Friday, and Pentecost. Green is for the weeks of Ordinary Time.

Activity

Color each chasuble the correct color for the church season or time of year.

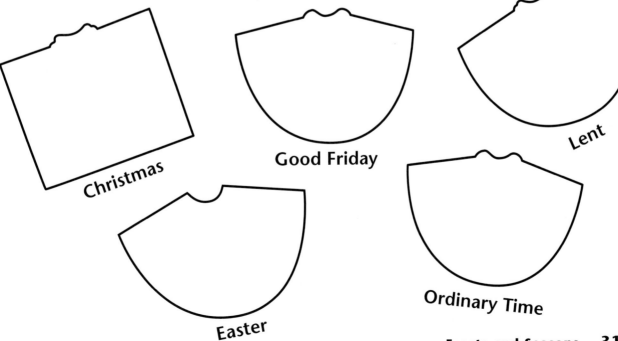

Advent

Christmas

Good Friday

Lent

Easter

Ordinary Time

Ordinary Time

Love God and love others as you love yourself.

Based on Luke 10:27

A Time to Learn

Ordinary Time is the longest part of the church year. Most weeks of Ordinary Time are in the summer and fall. The Sundays are counted in order. We say the Second Sunday in Ordinary Time, the Third Sunday, and so on.

The Gospel readings during Ordinary Time are about the life and teachings of Jesus. At Mass, we listen to stories of Jesus healing, blessing, and forgiving people. We learn ways to follow Jesus.

Activity

Look at the pictures of three Gospel stories that we hear at Mass during Ordinary Time. Write the number of each sentence in the correct box.

1. This picture shows Jesus teaching.

2. This picture shows Jesus blessing.

3. This picture shows Jesus healing.

Dear God, Thank you for the Gospel stories that teach us about Jesus. Help us to follow him each day. Amen.

Advent

Get ready to welcome the Lord!

Based on Isaiah 40:3

Welcome to Our Home!

Sometimes we welcome guests to our home. We want our guests to be happy. So we get ready to welcome them in special ways. A friendly welcome makes our guests feel special.

Activity

Circle the pictures that show some of the ways your family welcomes guests.

A Time to Get Ready

During **Advent** we get ready to welcome Jesus. We prepare our hearts. We do things for each other to show we care.

These are some of the ways our Church prepares us to welcome Jesus.

Each Sunday we light another candle on the Advent wreath.

We read Bible stories about people who waited for Jesus.

We care for those in need.

Jesus,
help me get ready
to welcome you.
Amen.

The Advent Wreath

God loves us and gives us many gifts. He even gives the gift of his Son, Jesus. This is the greatest gift of all.

An Advent wreath can help us get ready to welcome Jesus again. The one pink and three purple candles on the wreath form a circle.

As each candle is lit, we pray, "Come, Lord Jesus." The purple candles remind us to love and care for others. The pink candle reminds us to be happy because Christmas is near.

Activities

1. Complete each sentence below with a word from the box.

During Advent, we get ready to

_____

- -

welcome _____ .

_____

- -

There are _____ Sundays in Advent.

_____

- - - - - - - - - - - - - - - - - -

We _____ and care for others.

four
love
Jesus

2. Color the candles in the Advent wreath. Pray the Advent prayer.

"Come, Lord Jesus."

Lord, Jesus, I will be ready to welcome you. Amen.

The Visitation

"Yes, Angel Gabriel," Mary said. "Tell God that I will be the mother of his Son Jesus."

The angel said, "Your cousin Elizabeth is old. But God has granted her a baby, too. Her baby will be born soon."

Mary decided to visit her cousin. She wanted to tell Elizabeth her own good news. After a long walk, she arrived at her cousin's home. The women were happy to see each other. They talked about becoming mothers. They spoke about how wonderful God is.

Mary stayed with Elizabeth for a few months. She helped Elizabeth get ready for the birth of her baby. Then Mary went home to prepare for Jesus' birth.

Based on Luke 1:36–40, 46, 56

Activity

Many times our parents, grandparents, and teachers ask us to do things. These people love us and know what is good for us. We need to say "yes" to them just as Mary said "yes" to God.

What are some things grown-ups who love you might ask you to do?

Draw yourself doing one of these things.

Jesus, help me say "yes" to the people who love me and care for me. Amen.

✝ Prayer Celebration for Advent

We Prepare Our Hearts

All: Come, Lord Jesus,
Come, be with us.
Come, Lord Jesus, Maranatha!

Leader: Jesus, you came to show us how to live.
Help us prepare our hearts for you.
Help us show our love to others.

All: Amen.

Reader 1: Let us listen to the words of Mary's prayer. Mary said, "I praise the Lord with all my heart. I am happy about God my Savior. God all-powerful has done great things for me, and holy is his name."

Based on Luke 1:46–49

All: Come, Lord Jesus,
Come, be with us.
Come, Lord Jesus, Maranatha!

We Raise our hearts to Jesus.

We open our hearts to Jesus.

Leader: Let us lift our hearts in prayer. (*Pause.*) When we share our toys and talents,

All: We prepare our hearts for you, Jesus.

Reader 2: When we say kind words to someone,

All: We prepare our hearts for you, Jesus.

Reader 3: When we give food to hungry people,

All: We prepare our hearts for you, Jesus.

Child: When we (*Name a kind act*).

All: We prepare our hearts for you, Jesus.

Leader: Generous God, thank you for sending Jesus to be our Savior. Help us show our love to others during Advent and all year long.

All: Amen.

All: Come, Lord Jesus,
Come, be with us.
Come, Lord Jesus, Maranatha!

We prepare our hearts for Jesus.

We lift our hearts in prayer.

Christmas

 "The angel said, I have come from God to bring you Good News of great joy."

Based on Luke 2:10

A Promise

"Guess what? My big brother promised to play soccer with all of us," said Sammy.

Sammy is very excited. He wants his brother to keep his promise.

Activity

Draw a picture about a promise that you made to someone.

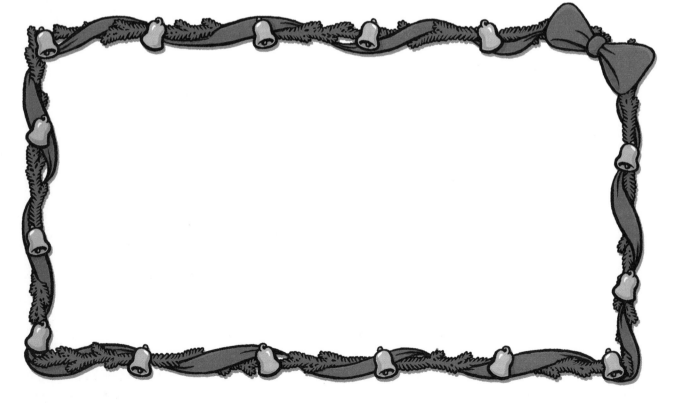

God Keeps a Promise

On **Christmas**, we gather at Mass. We listen carefully to the Gospel story of Jesus' birth.

Some shepherds were watching their sheep near Bethlehem. An angel sent by God appeared. The angel said, "Do not be afraid. I have come from God to bring you Good News. God has kept his promise. Today the Savior has been born. You will find him lying in a manger."

The shepherds ran and found Mary and Joseph. They found the Baby Jesus lying in a manger. The shepherds praised God for all they had seen.

Based on Luke 2:8–20

God our Father, thank you for keeping your promise and sending Jesus to be with us. Amen.

GLORY TO GOD PEACE ON EARTH

The Holy Family

The family of Jesus is called the Holy Family. Mary is Jesus' mother. Joseph is Mary's husband and Jesus' foster father. Jesus loved and obeyed Mary and Joseph. They were kind and caring to Jesus and to each other.

Feast of the Holy Family

During the Christmas season, we celebrate the Feast of the Holy Family. We celebrate the love that the members of the Holy Family have for each other. We honor God's love for all families.

Activities

1. Circle the correct answers.

What is the family of Jesus called?

the Holy Family   the Bethlehem Family

When is the Feast of the Holy Family?

in the summer   during the Christmas season

2. The words in the picture tell what families do to become holy. Color the words.

Holy Family,
help me be kind
and loving to each
person in my family.
Amen.

love

Share

help

Pray care

forgive

Prayer Celebration for Christmas

Silent Night

Leader: At Christmas, we think about the night Jesus was born.

Reader 1: We think about how much Mary and Joseph loved Baby Jesus.

Reader 2: We think about the shepherds, too.

Leader: It was very quiet and peaceful on that holy night. (*Pause.*)
Now let us sing "Silent Night."

All (*sing*): Silent night, holy night!
All is calm, all is bright.
'Round yon virgin, Mother and child.
Holy Infant so tender and mild;
Sleep in heavenly peace,
Sleep in heavenly peace.

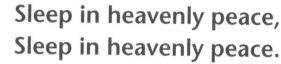

Leader: This is the story of "Silent Night." It was Christmas Eve in Austria over 200 years ago. The choir came to Saint Nicholas Church to practice for Midnight Mass. But the organ was broken.

Reader 3: Father Mohr said, "It won't seem like Christmas without music." Then he remembered a Christmas poem he had written called "Silent Night."

Reader 4: Franz Gruber, the organ player, said, "I'll write music for your poem." And he did.

Reader 5: Father Mohr played the music on his guitar. The choir learned to sing "Silent Night." They sang it at Midnight Mass. After Mass, everyone said,

All: **"The music was beautiful after all!"**

Leader: Let us pray silently for peace in the world. (*Pause.*)

Leader: Let us close our eyes and remember the first Christmas. (*Pause.*)
Now let us sing this holy song again.

All (*sing*): **Silent night, holy night! …**

Lent

"Come follow me!"

Based on John 1:43

Becoming More Like Jesus

Every day we try to become more like Jesus.
We are followers of Jesus. We are called to live
as Jesus showed us. We are called to love and
care for each other.

Activity

You are a follower of Jesus.
Draw yourself in the picture with
other followers of Jesus.

Forty Days

Lent lasts for forty days. During these forty days, we get ready to celebrate Easter. We try to become more like Jesus.

What Can We Do?

There are many things we can do during Lent to become more like Jesus. We can do some things with our parish community. We can do other things by ourselves.

With my parish community, I can

 sing at Mass on Sunday.

 care for the sick.

 pray for others.

By myself, I can

 be helpful to my family.

 obey my parents and teachers.

 forgive others.

Jesus, I want to be more like you. Help me to be kind and forgiving. Amen.

Ash Wednesday

Ash Wednesday is a special day that helps us get ready for Lent. We go to church. Ashes are rubbed on our foreheads in the shape of a cross. They remind us that we are followers of Jesus.

The cross reminds us that Jesus died to save us. It reminds us that he rose from the dead. The cross reminds us about Jesus' promise. He said that if we love God and others, we will be happy with God forever. This means that the cross is a sign of life.

Activities

1. Complete each sentence with a word from the box.

life
Ash
cross

_____

We get ready for Lent on _____ Wednesday.

Ashes are put on our foreheads in the

_____

shape of a _____.

_____

The cross is a sign of _____.

2. What does Jesus say to you? Trace the words to find out.

Come, follow me.

I pray always in the name of the Father, and of the Son, and of the Holy Spirit. Amen.

God's Promise

The Bible tells a story about Noah and a big flood. In the story, God sends water to flood the earth. Rain pours down for forty days. The rain almost washes everything away.

God saves Noah and his family from the flood. When the waters dry up, God makes a promise. God says that he will never let a flood destroy the earth again. Then God sends a rainbow as a sign of his promise.

Based on Genesis 9:8–15

Noah's Ark by Malcah Zeldis

New Life

Jesus promises his followers the gift of new life. At Baptism, we become members of the Church. The holy water of Baptism is a sign of our new life in Jesus.

Activity

Baptism life new brings

Write a sentence about Baptism with the words on the rainbow. Then color the rainbow.

_____

- -

_____

_____

- -

_____

_____

- -

_____.

Loving God, thank you for the gift of Baptism. I promise to follow Jesus always. Amen.

A Time for Prayer

During Lent, we remember that Jesus loves us. We remember that he wants us to be his followers.

Jesus was close to God, his Father. He prayed to God all the time. Jesus even prayed while he was on the cross.

We need to pray, too. We need to listen and talk to Jesus. When we pray, we grow closer to Jesus.

Activity

Make a prayer card for Jesus. Use words and pictures. Tell Jesus about something special that happened to you. Tell Jesus that you love him.

Dear Jesus,

Love,

Jesus, you show your love for me in so many ways. Let my prayers bring me closer to you. Amen.

Prayer Celebration for Lent

Baptism Makes Us New

Leader: Let us remember our Baptism. Through Baptism, we belong to the Catholic Church. We receive new life in Jesus.

Let us remember how much Jesus loves us. (*Pause.*)

Let us pray the Sign of the Cross.

All: In the name of the Father, and of the Son, and of the Holy Spirit. Amen.

Activity

Think about ways to follow Jesus during Lent. Share with a partner one way you are trying to be a follower of Jesus.

Leader: Let us pray an echo prayer. Like an echo, repeat the words you hear.

Reader 1: Jesus, teach us to be your followers.

All: (*Echo*)

Reader 2: We want to follow your way of truth.

All: (*Echo*)

Reader 3: We want to follow your way of goodness.

All: (*Echo*)

Reader 4: We want to follow your way of love.

All: (*Echo*)

Reader 5: We want to follow your ways of truth, goodness, and love.

All: (*Echo*)

Based on Psalm 25:4–6

Share your toys.

Leader: Jesus, we will always follow you. (*Pause.*)

All: Yes, Jesus, we will always follow you.

Forgive others.

Holy Week

Blessed is the king who comes in the name of the Lord.

Luke 19:38

Palm Sunday

The first day of Holy Week is called Palm Sunday. It is the Sunday before Easter. We remember how Jesus came into Jerusalem.

Activity

Read the story below.
Use the pictures to help you.

Palms are branches of .

Palm trees grow in hot, places.

One day a crowd of cheered and waved palms.

The people were happy to see .

They had a great parade to honor Jesus.

Palm Sunday Mass

At Mass on Palm Sunday, we hold palm branches. We listen to the Gospel story about Jesus going into the city of Jerusalem. We hear how the joyful crowd welcomes Jesus by shouting "Hosanna!"

We walk into church with the priest and our parish community. Like the people of Jerusalem, we say, "Blessed is the king who comes in the name of the Lord." (Luke 19:38).

After Mass, we take our palm branches home. We welcome Jesus into our hearts and homes.

Lord Jesus, we shout "Hosanna!" We welcome you as our king. Amen.

Three Holy Days

The three days before Easter Sunday are Holy Thursday, Good Friday, and Holy Saturday. These three days are very holy.

On Holy Thursday, we remember the Last Supper. At the Last Supper, Jesus changed bread and wine into his Body and Blood. This is how Jesus gave us the Sacrament of the Eucharist.

On Good Friday, we remember that Jesus died for us. This day is called Good Friday because it is good that Jesus saved us from sin.

On Holy Saturday night, we celebrate that Jesus was raised from the dead. We begin to celebrate Easter, the Church's greatest feast.

Activity

Complete each sentence with a word from the box.

Saturday   Friday   Thursday

Jesus gave us the Eucharist at the Last Supper. We remember this on

_____

- -

Holy _____.

Jesus died on the cross to save us from sin. We remember this on

_____

- -

Good _____.

The Easter celebration begins at night on

_____

- -

Holy _____.

Jesus, our Savior, we give you thanks for everything you did for us. Amen.

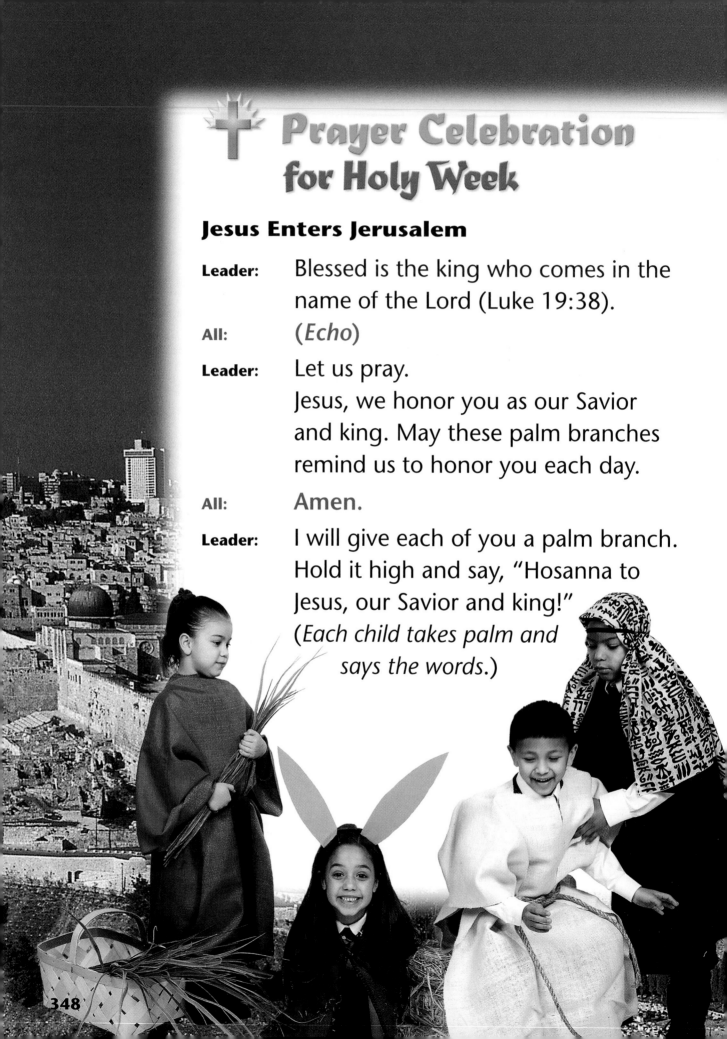

Prayer Celebration for Holy Week

Jesus Enters Jerusalem

Leader: Blessed is the king who comes in the name of the Lord (Luke 19:38).

All: (*Echo*)

Leader: Let us pray.
Jesus, we honor you as our Savior and king. May these palm branches remind us to honor you each day.

All: Amen.

Leader: I will give each of you a palm branch. Hold it high and say, "Hosanna to Jesus, our Savior and king!" (*Each child takes palm and says the words.*)

A Gospel Play for Palm Sunday

Friend 1: Jesus, we are almost there. I can see Jerusalem. I can see the city gates.

Jesus: Go find a donkey and bring it to me.

Friend 2: What if someone asks why I am taking the donkey?

Jesus: Just say, "The Lord needs it."

(*The friends go and find a donkey.*)

Owner: Why are you taking my donkey?

Friend 1: The Lord needs it.

(*The friends bring the donkey to Jesus.*)

Friend 2: Let us help you get on the donkey.

Jesus: Thank you. Now let us go.

Friend 1: The people see us. They are waving palm branches. Listen to them.

People: (*Hold up palm.*) Blessed is the king who comes in the name of the Lord.

Based on the Lectionary for Masses with Children

All: Hosanna to Jesus, our Savior and king!

Easter

I have seen the Lord. He is alive!

Based on John 20:18

Signs of Spring

Imagine that it is Sunday afternoon.
You are taking a walk with your family.
The sun is shining. The breeze feels warm.
The air smells fresh and clean. You see
many signs of new life.
You are very happy
that spring is here.

Activity

Look at the picture.
Circle the signs of
new life that you see.

Jesus Is Alive!

Jesus died on a cross. His followers were very sad. They felt scared and all alone. They missed Jesus very much. Three days later, God raised Jesus from the dead. God gave Jesus the gift of new life. Jesus' friends were filled with joy. The Risen Jesus was with them again. They thanked God for raising Jesus to new life.

We Celebrate Easter

Easter is our greatest feast. We celebrate Jesus' new life. We believe that we will share new life with Jesus forever. On Easter Sunday, we go to Mass. We sing joyful songs. We pray joyful prayers. We say "Alleluia!"

The Resurrection by Ditlev Knutson

Risen Jesus,
help us share in your
new life. Alleluia!
Amen.

Jesus Appears to Mary of Magdala

Mary of Magdala was a follower of Jesus. She went to visit the tomb where he was buried. But the tomb was empty.

More of Jesus' followers came to the place. After seeing the empty tomb, they went home.

Mary of Magdala was sad and upset. She stayed beside the tomb. She heard a man's voice. He asked, "Why are you crying?"

At first Mary thought the man was the gardener. But when he said "Mary," she knew that he was Jesus.

Mary hurried to tell everyone that she had seen the Risen Jesus.

Based on John 20:1–16

Risen Christ Appears to Mary Magdalene by Martin Schongauer

Activity

Use the words in the box to complete the sentences.

Risen	Mary	empty	Jesus

Mary of Magdala saw the

_____

_____ tomb.

_____

_____ appeared

to Mary of Magdala.

Mary told others that she had seen the

_____

_____ Jesus.

_____

_____ said, "Jesus is alive."

Mary of Magdala,
help me share the
good news of Jesus'
rising from the dead.
Amen. Alleluia!

Jesus Ascends to Heaven

Jesus knew that it was time for him to leave the earth. He needed to return to God, his Father.

Forty days after Easter, Jesus spoke to his Apostles. He told them to go all over the world to share the Good News of the Gospel. Then the Apostles saw Jesus ascend to Heaven.

We celebrate Jesus' return to his Father on a special feast day. It is called the Feast of the Ascension. This feast is sometimes called Ascension Thursday.

The Ascension by Jean Fouquet

Activity

Jesus' Apostles saw him ascend to heaven.
What does the word *ascend* mean?

Cross out each block with the letter **Z** on it.
Then write the sentence that is left over.
Begin with the word at the bottom.

_____

- -

_____

- -

_____ .

Jesus, God raised
you up to new life. We
believe that we will live
with you forever.
Amen. Alleluia!

Prayer Celebration for Easter

We Rejoice

Leader: Let us raise our hearts and minds to God. Let us joyfully sing together.

All (sing): Christ has died.
Christ is risen.
Christ will come again.

Relax

Leader: Close your eyes and breathe slowly.
Breathe in: 1, 2, 3, 4, 5
Hold your breath: 1, 2, 3
Breathe out: 1, 2, 3, 4, 5

Look and Think

Look at the picture of the empty tomb. See how the stone is rolled back. Be still and think about the Risen Jesus.

Imagine

Imagine that you are sitting alone at the empty tomb. All of a sudden, Jesus appears beside you. He calls you by name. You sit and talk to Jesus. You listen to him.

Pray

Leader: Let us pray to the Risen Jesus.

Side 1: Risen Jesus, we believe you are alive.

Side 2: We believe you are with us.

Side 1: Help us see you in other people.

Side 2: Help us show our love to others.

All: Even to those we do not like.

Leader: Risen Jesus, we are glad you are alive!

All: Alleluia! Alleluia!

Holy Days

 Happy are you who love God and walk
in his ways.

Based on Psalm 128:1

Guardian Angels

God gives every person a guardian angel.
Guardian angels protect us and guide us.
They try to keep us from harm.

You can tell your guardian angel when you
are afraid. You can tell your guardian angel
when you find it hard to do what is good.
Your guardian angel will pray for you and
tell God about your needs.

We celebrate the Feast of the Guardian
Angels on October 2.

A Guardian Angel Prayer

You can say a special prayer called "Angel of God." It begins like this.

Angel of God, my guardian dear, to whom God's love commits me here.

This means that God puts you in the care of your guardian angel.

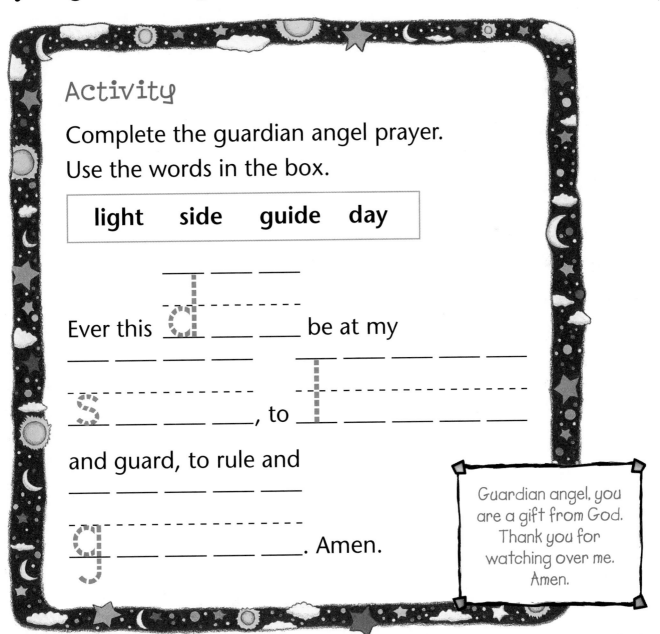

Activity

Complete the guardian angel prayer.
Use the words in the box.

light	side	guide	day

Ever this d _ _ _ _ be at my

_ _ _ _ _ _ _ _ _ _ _ _ _ _

s _ _ _ _, to l _ _ _ _ _

and guard, to rule and

_ _ _ _ _ _ _ _

g _ _ _ _ _. Amen.

Guardian angel, you are a gift from God. Thank you for watching over me. Amen.

All Saints Day

November 1 is the Feast of All Saints. On that day we go to Mass.

Saints are holy people who loved God and showed their love for others. Some even died for their belief in God.

Many saints have a special feast day when the Church honors them. Other saints are not famous or well known. Some lived very quiet lives. They do not have their own special feast day.

On All Saints Day, the Church honors every saint.

All Saints in Heaven from the *Book of Hours*, Belgium, c.1440

Listening to God's Word

The Gospel reading on the Feast of All Saints tells us how we should live. It tells us to trust in God. It tells us to forgive and to care for others. This Gospel tells us to be people of peace.

Activities

1. Circle the words that best complete each sentence.

   On the Feast of All Saints, we _____.

   go to Mass   **visit Grandpa**

   The Gospel on All Saints Day tells us to _____.

   forget about others   **trust in God**

2. Draw about a time when you helped someone.

Loving God,
may our hearts be full
of love like the hearts
of the saints who are
with you. Amen.

All Souls Day

November 2 is All Souls Day. On this day, we pray for all the people who died. We remember the good things they did on earth. We know that they tried to be good. We pray that they are with God in Heaven. Here is our prayer.

"May the angels lead them into Heaven. May the saints come to welcome them. And may they praise God forever in his Kingdom."

Based on Order of Christian Funerals

Activity

What do you think Mary was like when she was six years old? Make a birthday card for the young Mary. Write your own birthday greeting.

Mary, I want to be a good and holy child, as you were. Please pray for me. Amen.

Mary, the Mother of God

God chose Mary to be the mother of his Son Jesus. We call Mary the Mother of God. Mary is very special.

Mary cared for Jesus. Jesus wants Mary to love and care for us, too. He gave her to us as our special mother. She loves us and cares for us. Mary prays for us. She tells Jesus about our needs.

We celebrate the Feast of Mary, the Mother of God on January 1.

Activities

1. How do you think Mary took care of Jesus?
Draw a picture that shows your thoughts.

2. Mary is your mother, too. How can she help you?

_____

- -

_____

_____

- -

_____

Mary, Mother of God
and our mother, too,
help our love for your
Son, Jesus, grow.
Amen.

The Month of May

During the month of May, Catholics honor Mary in special ways. Many Catholic schools honor her with a May procession.

Each child brings a small plant with flowers. The children line up, holding their plants. The procession begins with a hymn to honor Mary. The children slowly walk to the statue of Mary. One-by-one, they place their plants around the statue. Together they pray the Hail Mary.

OUR CATHOLIC HERITAGE

What Catholics Believe

How Catholics Worship

How Catholics Live

How Catholics Pray

WHAT CATHOLICS BELIEVE

We can learn about our faith from the Bible and from the teachings of the Church.

ABOUT
THE BIBLE

The Bible is a special book about God. Some stories in the Bible tell how God loves and cares for people. Other stories tell about Jesus and his followers.

God chose many people to write the Bible. We believe that the Bible is the Word of God.

You can learn more about the Bible on pages 17–21 and in Chapter 3.

ABOUT
THE TRINITY

We believe that there is only one God.
We believe that there is one God in Three Persons.
The Three Persons are God the Father,
God the Son, and God the Holy Spirit.
We call the Three Persons the **Holy Trinity**.

We Believe in God the Father

God the Father created the world. He created all of us. Everything God made shows his love.

We are God's children. Like a loving father, God watches over us. He wants us to take care of the world. God wants us to care for each other.

We Believe in God the Son

The Son of God the Father became man. His name is Jesus. He lived on earth to teach us how to love his Father and one another.

Jesus died on the cross and rose from the dead. He saved us from sin. Jesus Christ is our Savior.

We Believe in God the Holy Spirit

The Holy Spirit is God. He is the gift of the love of God the Father and God the Son. The Holy Spirit is always with us.

The Holy Spirit gives us grace to help us follow Jesus. Grace is God's loving presence in our lives.

ABOUT THE CATHOLIC CHURCH

We belong to the Catholic Church. We are called Catholics. We are followers of Jesus.

The Pope is the leader of the Catholic Church all over the world. He lives in Rome. We call the Pope our Holy Father.

A bishop is the leader of a diocese. A diocese is made up of many parishes. A bishop teaches and cares for the people of his diocese.

A priest serves the people of a parish. He celebrates Mass with the parish community. He teaches people about the Good News of Jesus. A priest needs many helpers to care for all the people in the parish.

ambo

candle →

ABOUT
A VISIT TO CHURCH

A Catholic church is a very special place to visit.

We go to church to worship God. We go to church to celebrate Mass with our parish community.

Look at the picture. It shows some things that we can see in our parish church.

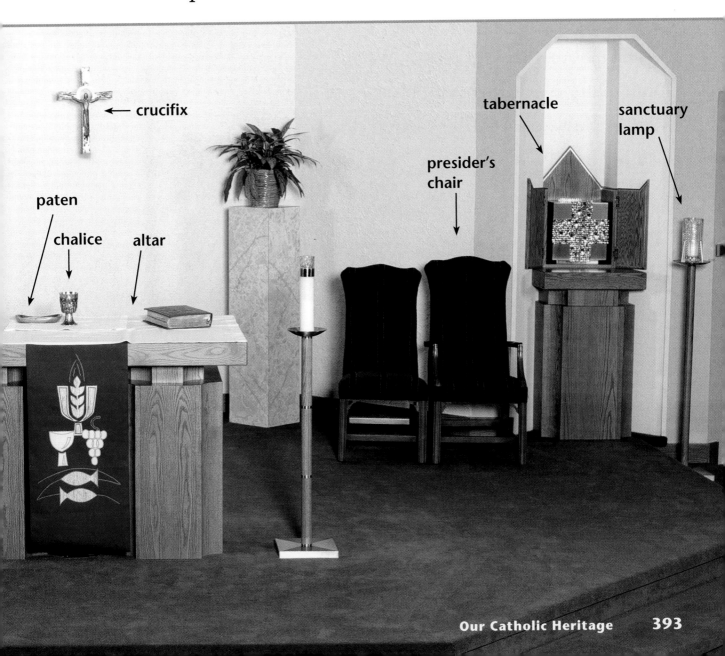

crucifix

tabernacle

sanctuary lamp

presider's chair

paten

chalice

altar

ABOUT
MARY

Mary was good and holy. God chose her to be the mother of his Son, Jesus. Mary loved and trusted God. She loved and cared for Jesus.

Mary is our mother, too. Like a good mother, Mary loves and cares for us.

Mary is our greatest **saint**. We honor Mary by calling her "Mother of God." We ask Mary, the Mother of God, to pray for us.

ABOUT
NEW LIFE FOREVER

Jesus teaches us how to love God and others. Jesus says that if we act with love, we will have new life. Jesus promises that if we love God and others, we will live forever.

When we die, we will be with Jesus, Mary, and all the good and holy people who ever lived. Happiness with God forever is called Heaven.

394

HOW CATHOLICS WORSHIP

Worship is giving honor and praise to God. We worship when we pray and when we celebrate the Sacraments.

ABOUT THE SACRAMENTS

The Sacraments are celebrations of God's love for us. We celebrate that we are followers of Jesus Christ. We celebrate that we share in his new life.

Baptism is the Sacrament of welcome into the Church. At Baptism, we become children of God. The water of Baptism washes away all sin and fills us with God's grace.

Confirmation is the Sacrament in which the Holy Spirit makes our faith in Christ stronger. The Holy Spirit helps us share the Good News of Jesus.

The **Eucharist** is the Sacrament in which Jesus Christ shares himself with us. We receive the Body and Blood of Christ.

Penance and Reconciliation is the Sacrament of forgiveness. We say that we are sorry for our sins. We celebrate God's forgiveness.

Anointing of the Sick is the Sacrament that brings the peace of Jesus to people who are sick.

Holy Orders is the Sacrament that celebrates the mission of deacons, priests, and bishops. These men are called to serve God's people in a special way.

Matrimony is the Sacrament that celebrates the love of a baptized man and a baptized woman for each other. They promise to be faithful to each other their whole life. They are ready to begin their family life.

ABOUT THE MASS

1. Our celebration begins. The priest and other ministers go to the altar. We stand and sing a welcome song.

2. We make the Sign of the Cross. The priest welcomes us with these words: "The Lord be with you."

3. We remember our sins. We ask God to forgive us.

4. We listen to the Word of God in readings from the Bible. After each of the first two readings we say "Thanks be to God."

5. The priest or deacon reads the Gospel story. The word *gospel* means "good news." We stand and listen to the Good News story of Jesus. We say "Praise to you, Lord Jesus Christ."

6. The priest or deacon helps us understand Jesus' message in a special talk called the homily.

7. In the Prayer of the Faithful, we ask God to help the Church, our country, and all of God's people.

8. We bring the gifts of bread and wine to the altar for the holy meal with Jesus. We remember that Jesus always loves us.

9. The priest blesses God and offers him our gifts of bread and wine. We say, "Blessed be God for ever."

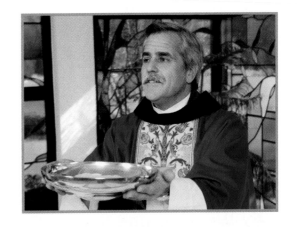

10. We thank and praise God for all of our blessings. We especially thank God for the gift of Jesus.

11. The priest prays as Jesus did at the Last Supper. Our gifts of bread and wine become the Body and Blood of Jesus Christ.

12. The priest holds up the Body and Blood of Jesus. He says a prayer to praise God. We answer "Amen."

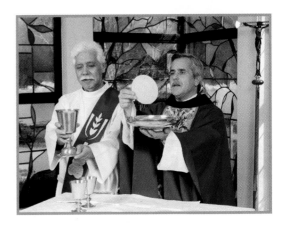

13. We say the "Lord's Prayer." This is the prayer that Jesus taught us to say.

14. We offer one another a Sign of Peace. This is a sign that reminds us to live as Jesus teaches us to live.

15. We receive Jesus in the Eucharist. Sharing Jesus' Body and Blood in a special way means that we are promising to follow Jesus.

16. We receive God's blessing. We answer "Amen." We sing a song of praise. We go in peace to love and serve God and one another.

HOW CATHOLICS LIVE

Jesus teaches us how to live. He gives us the Holy Spirit and the Church to help us.

ABOUT
THE GREAT COMMANDMENT

God's laws are really one Great Commandment. Jesus said, "You must love God above all things and love your neighbor as yourself" (based on Mark 12:30–31). The Great Commandment tells us how to love God and other people.

ABOUT
THE NEW COMMANDMENT

Jesus gave us a New Commandment. He said, "Love one another as I have loved you" (based on John 13:34). We show our love for others when we are helpful and kind.

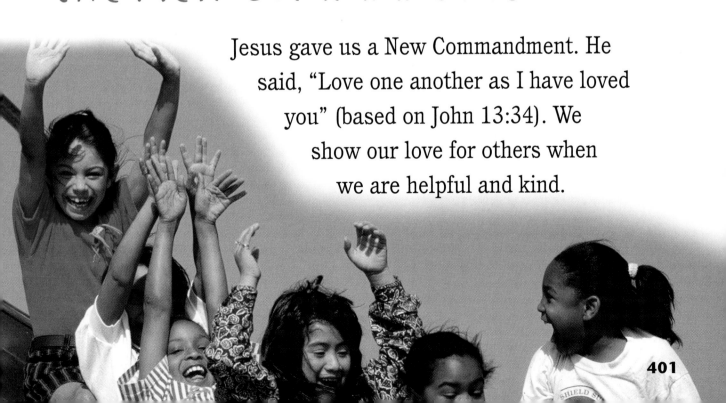

ABOUT

THE TEN COMMANDMENTS

The Ten Commandments are God's laws, or rules, that tell us
how to show our love for God, ourselves, and other people.

God's Laws	We live God's Laws
1. I am the LORD your God: you shall not have strange gods before me.	We belive in God and love God.
2. You shall not take the name of the LORD your God in vain.	We use God's name with love.
3. Remember to keep holy the LORD's Day.	We celebrate Mass with our parish community. We keep the Lord's Day holy.
4. Honor your father and your mother.	We obey our parents and those who care for us.
5. You shall not kill.	We care for all living things.
6. You shall not commit adultery.	We respect our bodies and the bodies of others.
7. You shall not steal.	We respect what is given to us and what belongs to others.
8. You shall not bear false witness against your neighbor.	We always tell the truth.
9. You shall not covet your neighbor's wife.	We rejoice in the happiness of others.
10. You shall not covet your neighbor's goods.	We do not want more than we need.

Based on Exodus 20:2–17

ABOUT
SIN AND FORGIVENESS

Sin is a choice to do something that we know is wrong. Sin is turning away from God. Sin hurts our friendship with people.

We know that God loves us. We know that he is always ready to forgive us. God wants us to be sorry for our sins. He wants us to promise to do better. We can ask the Holy Spirit to help us.

✝ Dear God,
I am sorry for what I did wrong. I will try to do better. I will love and care for others. Please send the Holy Spirit to help me.
Amen.

Jesus teaches us to love and care for others. Sometimes people do wrong things to us. We should always be ready to forgive them. We can say "I forgive you."

ABOUT
VOCATIONS

We become members of the Catholic Church at Baptism. God calls us to love him and serve him in a special way. This is called our vocation.

Religious Vocations

God calls some people to a special life of service in the Church. The call to be a priest, deacon, and religious sister or brother is called a religious vocation.

Many priests serve the Church by being leaders of parish communities. Others teach or work with poor people.

Deacons help the priests in parishes. They lead celebrations of Baptism and marriage. At Mass, they teach people about the Bible readings. Deacons visit the sick and pray with families of people who have died.

Let us pray that more men and women will answer God's call to a religious vocation.

Many religious sisters and brothers serve in parishes. Some work in schools and hospitals. Others share the Good News of Jesus with poor people all over the world.

Other Calls to Serve

God calls all Catholics to serve the Church. Some Catholics help at Mass. They welcome the people. They read aloud from the Bible. They lead the singing of holy songs. They help give Holy Communion to the people.

Other Catholics teach children and adults about God's love. They share the Good News about Jesus. They teach people to pray in different ways.

Many Catholics visit the sick and help the poor. They give money to help people in need.

As you grow up, God will call you to serve the Church in special ways. Will you be ready to say yes to his call?

HOW CATHOLICS PRAY

Prayer is talking and listening to God. We can pray anywhere and at any-time. God is everywhere. God always hears our prayers.

ABOUT
KINDS OF PRAYER

There are many different ways to pray. We can say the prayers we learn at home and in church. We can use our own words to pray, too. Sometimes we can just be quiet in God's presence. We do not even have to say any words.

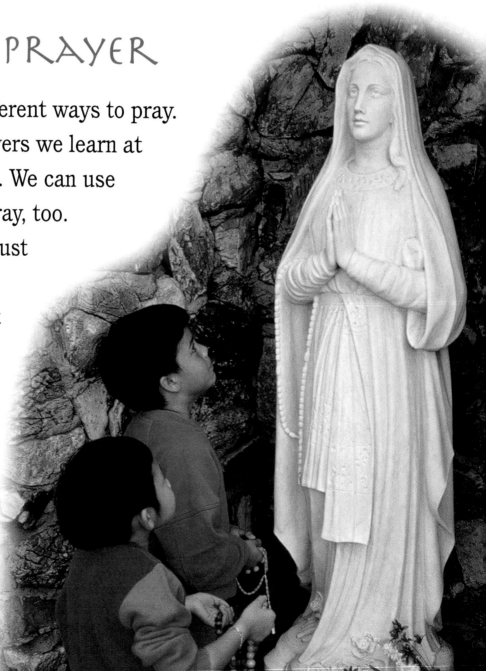

The children are praying the Rosary to honor Mary.

Our thoughts can be a prayer. Our hopes can be a prayer. This kind of prayer is called meditation. In meditation we use our imagination to think about God. We think about what God wants us to do.

We can use our bodies when we pray. When we make the Sign of the Cross, we use our hands. Sometimes we kneel when we pray. We can even sing or dance as a prayer to God.

We are never alone when we pray. God always hears our prayers.

ABOUT
THE LORD'S PRAYER

The Lord's Prayer is a very special prayer. Jesus taught us the words. In this prayer, Jesus teaches us to call God "Our Father." We believe that God is everyone's loving Father.

Our Father, who art in heaven, hallowed be thy name;
  God is our Father. We praise God's holy name.

thy kingdom come;
  We pray that everyone will know God's love and live in peace.

thy will be done on earth as it is in heaven.
  We pray that everyone will follow God's law.

Give us this day our daily bread;
  We pray for our needs and the needs of others.

and forgive us our trespasses as we forgive those who trespass against us;
  We ask God to forgive us when we sin.
  We remember that we must forgive others.

and lead us not into temptation,
  We ask God to help us make good choices.

but deliver us from evil.
  We pray that God will protect us from harm.

Amen.
  "Amen" means that we believe the words we say.

CELEBRATING CATHOLIC SCHOOLS WEEK

CATHOLIC SCHOOLS IN AMERICA
The First Catholic School Teacher

Missionaries

Long ago, priests called missionaries came to California from Spain. The native people helped them build churches and schools in villages called missions.

The missionaries taught the native people about Jesus. Many became Catholic. They taught the people how to read and write. The missionaries also taught them new ways to farm and care for animals. They were the first Catholic school teachers in America.

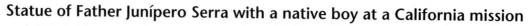

Statue of Father Junípero Serra with a native boy at a California mission

Mission San Antonio

Father Serra and two other priests started Mission San Antonio. The picture shows how the mission looked about 200 years ago.

Activity

Listen to a story by a boy at the mission. Point to each part of the picture as you hear about it in the story.

CATHOLIC SCHOOLS TODAY

Loving and Learning Communities

Catholic schools today welcome all children. They are safe and friendly communities where children learn, share, and care for others.

The children in one Catholic school were asked what they like about their school. Amanda said, "I feel like I'm part of a family. I like the hands-on science program because it's so much fun that I hardly know I'm learning." Chris said, "The teachers are kind and helpful. I like learning about Jesus' life. I have fun doing holiday projects and going on field trips." Grace said, "I'm learning to share the gifts God has given me. I like my teachers because they take time to answer my questions."

? What do you like about your school?

We care about the world.

A Catholic School Community

Many people make up a Catholic school community. There are teachers, children, and parents. There is a pastor, a principal, a school nurse, and a custodian. There are also lunchroom helpers and teacher aides.

Activity

In each frame, draw a person who belongs to your school community. Write each person's name in the space above.

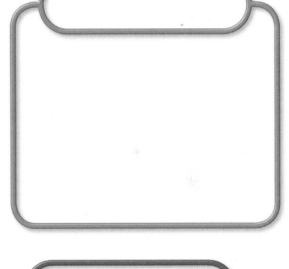

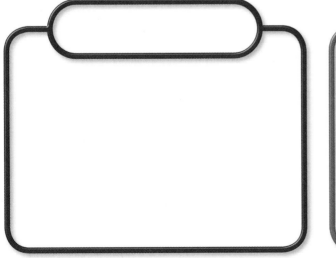

MY CATHOLIC SCHOOL

A Scavenger Hunt

A scavenger hunt is a game in which people are sent to find things. When the things are found, the people report back to the group.

Activity

- Go on a scavenger hunt. Find six things that show you are in a Catholic school.

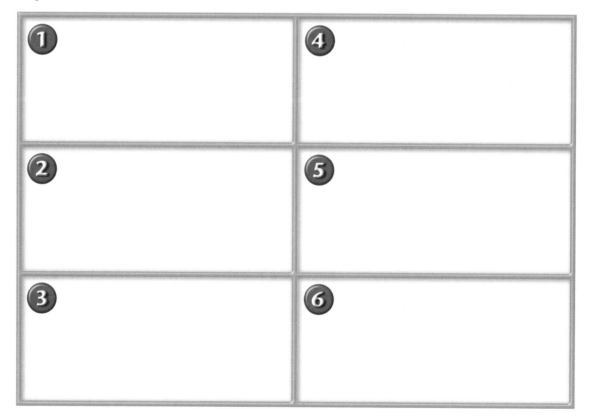

- Draw or write the name of each thing you find on the chart below.

①	④
②	⑤
③	⑥

What I like About My School

Complete the
sentences.

1. The name of my school is

_____

- -

_____.

2. I like my school because

_____

- -

_____

_____

- -

_____.

3. Two children in my class are

_____

- -

_____

_____

- -

_____.

4. My favorite thing to do in school is

_____

- -

_____.

Prayer Celebration for Catholic Schools Week

Giving Thanks for Teachers

Leader: The early missionaries were teachers who had great faith and courage. Let us thank God for these first teachers.

All: We thank you, God.

Side 1: Let us thank God for the teachers in our school.

Side 2: We thank you, God.

ABCDEFGH
NOPQRSTU

Jesus

Side 1: Let us tell God that we will work hard in school.

Side 2: Loving God, we will work hard. We will try to do our best.

Leader: God, our Father, your Son Jesus taught us how to live. Help us follow his example. We ask this in Jesus' name.

All: Amen.

MY FIRST GRADE FAVORITES

My favorite Bible story is

_____

- - - - - - - - - - - - - - - - -

_____

_____

- - - - - - - - - - - - - - - - -

_____

_____

- - - - - - - - - -

on page _____.

My favorite activity is

_____

- - - - - - - - - -

on page _____.

My favorite Bible people are

_____

- - - - - - - - - - - - - - - - -

_____

- - - - - - - - - - - - - - - - -

_____

My favorite holy person is

_____

- - - - - - - - - - - - - - - - -

_____

My favorite saints are

_____

- - - - - - - - - - - - - - - - - - - -

_____

_____

_____

My favorite picture of Jesus is on page

_____

- - - - - - - - - - - - -

_____.

My favorite way to pray is on page

_____

- - - - - - - - - - - - -

_____.

My favorite things in church are

My favorite holy song is on page

_____

- - - - - - - - - - - - -

_____.

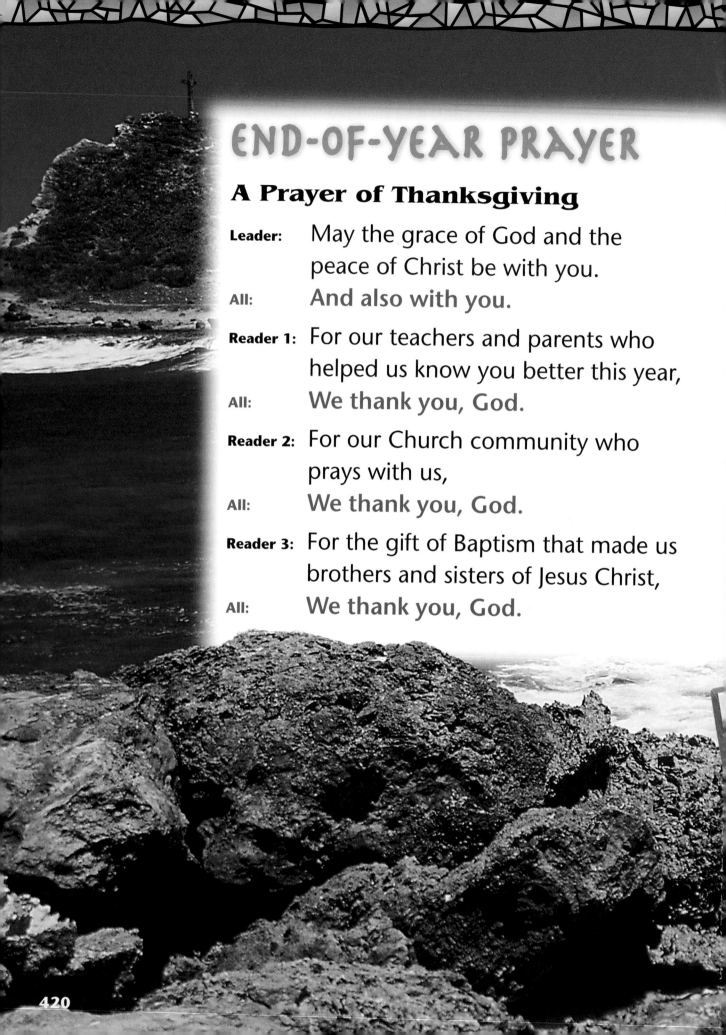

END-OF-YEAR PRAYER

A Prayer of Thanksgiving

Leader: May the grace of God and the peace of Christ be with you.

All: And also with you.

Reader 1: For our teachers and parents who helped us know you better this year,

All: We thank you, God.

Reader 2: For our Church community who prays with us,

All: We thank you, God.

Reader 3: For the gift of Baptism that made us brothers and sisters of Jesus Christ,

All: We thank you, God.

Reader 4: For the gift of your Son Jesus,

All: We thank you, God.

Reader 5: For the gift of the Holy Spirit,

All: We thank you, God.

Reader 6: For all the good times we had in first grade,

All: We thank you, God.

Leader: May our lives be blessed this summer and always, in the name of the Father and of the Son and of the Holy Spirit.

All: Amen.

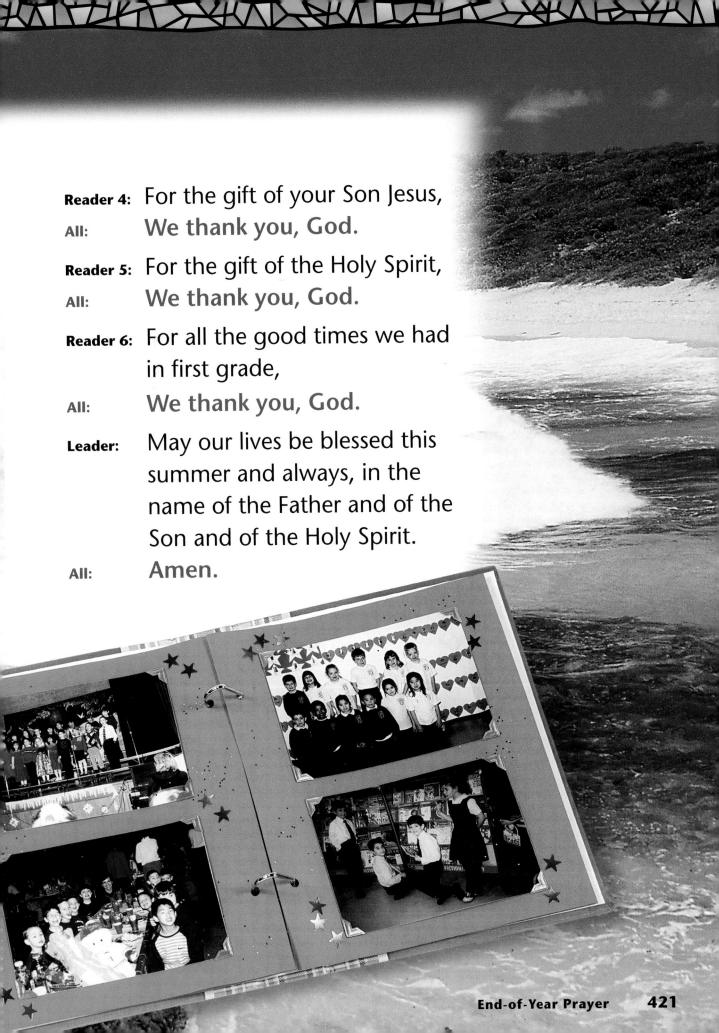

Write-in Glossary

adore
(page 162)

To _____ Jesus Christ means "to worship or honor him as the Son of God."

Advent
(page 321)

_____ is the time before Christmas when we get ready to welcome Jesus into our lives.

Amen
(page 263)

_____ means "Yes, I believe. It is true." We often say "Amen" at the end of prayers.

angel
(pages 145, 358)

An _____ is a helper or a messenger from God. Guardian angels protect and guide us.

Anointing of the Sick
(page 396)

_____ of the _____ is a Sacrament that brings the peace of Christ to people who are sick.

Baptism
(pages 99, 217)

The Sacrament of _____ is a celebration of welcome into the Catholic community.

Bible
(page 53)

The _____ is the written Word of God. God chose special people to write the Bible.

Blessed Sacrament
(page 160)

The _____ is another name for the Eucharist.

blessing
(page 46)

A _____ is a gift from God. It can also be a prayer that asks for God's protection and care.

Catholic Church
(page 31)

The _____ is the community of Jesus' followers to which we belong.

Christ
(page 159)

_____ is another name for Jesus. It tells us that he was sent by God to save all people.

Christians
(page 226)

_____ are people who love Jesus Christ and follow him.

Christmas
(page 329)

_____ is the time when we celebrate the birth of Jesus.

church
(page 40)

A _____ is a special place where Catholics come together to pray.

community
(page 31)

A _____ is a group of people who belong together.

Confirmation
(page 217)

_____ is the sacrament in which the Holy Spirit makes our faith in Jesus Christ stronger.

Creation
(page 87)

_____ is everything that God made.

Creator
(page 89)

God is our _____. God made everything in the world.

Eucharist
(page 157)

The _____ is the holy meal that Jesus shares with us at Mass. The bread and wine become the Body and Blood of Jesus Christ.

faith
(page 261)

Our _____ is our belief and trust in God.

forgive
(page 169)

The word _____ means "to excuse or to pardon."

Fruits of the Holy Spirit
(page 227)

The _____ of the _____

_____

_____ are signs that the Holy Spirit is acting in our lives. Some fruits are love, joy, peace, patience, gentleness, kindness, and self-control.

Gloria
(page 68)

The _____ is a prayer of praise to God. It is often said or sung at Mass.

Gospel
(page 183)

The _____ is the Good News of Jesus. There are four Gospels in the Bible.

grace
(page 101)

The gift of _____ is God's loving presence in our lives.

hallowed
(page 125)

The word _____ means "holy."

Heaven
(page 111)

_____ is happiness with God forever.

holy
(page 111)

To be _____ means "to be like God."

Holy Orders
(page 396)

The Sacrament of _____ celebrates God's call to become a deacon, priest, or bishop.

Holy Spirit
(page 203)

The _____ is God. The Holy Spirit helps us follow Jesus.

Holy Trinity
(page 390)

The _____ is one God in Three Persons—God the Father, God the Son, and God the Holy Spirit.

hymn
(page 297)

A _____ is a holy song that lifts our hearts to God.

Jesus
(page 147)

_____ is the Son of God.

Joseph
(pages 147, 330)

_____ is Mary's husband and the foster father of Jesus.

Last Supper
(page 157)

The _____ is the holy meal that Jesus shared with his friends on the night before he died.

Lord's Prayer
(page 125)

The _____ is the prayer that Jesus taught us.

Matrimony
(page 396)

The Sacrament of _____ celebrates the love that a man and woman have for each other.

Mary
(page 145)

_____ is the Mother of Jesus.

Mass
(pages 40, 157)

The _____ is the celebration of the holy meal that Jesus shares with us.

mercy
(page 174)

God's _____ is his loving forgiveness. We are called to show mercy to others.

mission
(page 285)

Our _____ as Christians is to love and serve others.

parish
(page 43)

A _____ is a group of Catholics who belong to the same church community.

Pentecost
(page 273)

_____ celebrates the coming of the Holy Spirit and the birthday of the Church.

petition
(page 239)

A _____ is an asking prayer. We ask God for the things we need.

praise
(page 65)

A prayer of _____ celebrates God's goodness.

Prayer
(page 65)

_____ is listening to and talking to God.

Psalms
(page 181)

_____ are prayers from the Bible that people often sing. The Book of Psalms is in the Bible.

Reconciliation
(page 396)

_____ is the Sacrament that celebrates God's forgiveness.

Sacraments
(page 215)

The _____ are special signs of God's love.

saint
(page 394)

A _____ is a special person who lived a holy life. The life of a saint shows us how to follow Jesus.

Savior
(page 147)

Our _____ is Jesus, the Son of God. He helps us and saves us.

serve
(page 285)

To _____ means "to help other people."

sin
(page 171)

To _____ is to choose to do something that we know is wrong.

tabernacle
(pages 158, 159)

A _____ is a container in church where the Blessed Sacrament is kept.

Temple
(page 180)

The _____ was a special building in Jerusalem. Jesus prayed in the Temple and learned about God.

Index